TRIC-TRAC

G. E. S.

TRIC-TRAC

by

Charlotte Grey

Dales Large Print Books
Long Preston, North Yorkshire,
BD23 4ND, England.

British Library Cataloguing in Publication Data.

Grey, Charlotte
    Tric-trac.

        A catalogue record of this book is
        available from the British Library

        ISBN   978-1-84262-593-4 pbk

First published in Great Britain in 2003 by The Book Guild Ltd.

Published in Large Print 2008 by arrangement with
Book Guild Publishing

Dales Large Print is an imprint of Library Magna Books Ltd.

Printed and bound in Great Britain by
T.J. (International) Ltd., Cornwall, PL28 8RW

I earn that I eat,
get that I wear;
owe no man hate,
envy no man's happiness,
glad of other men's good,
content with my harm;
and the greatest of my pride is,
to see my ewes graze and my lambs suck.

William Shakespeare, *As You Like It*, III, 2

CONTENTS

GLOSSARY

aa all
a'b'dy everybody
ain own
amang amongst
auld old
ava at all
awa away
aye ever, always

baith both
bawbee small coin
baud hare
beese beasts
bield shelter
blaws blows
brak broke
braw beautiful
bricht bright
brig, **briggie** bridge

cairt cart

capercaillie large European grouse
cauldrife cold
cawfie calf
chokit choked
coorse coarse
couthy pleasant, nice

dae do
deen done
dees dies
dochter daughter
dool woe
doot doubt
dreich dreary
drouth thirst
dunt a blow, knock
dyke-lowper a jumper (over wall)

een, eence one, once
eneuch enough
erse arse

fairing getting ready
fecht fight
fin when
fit like?, foo's yersel' how are you?
frae from
fu' full, drunk
futtrat ferret, weasel

gey very
gied gave
gweed good

haar thick mist
heich high
heid head
hev, hiv have
howd o'wind strong wind

ides 15th day
ilka each, every
ingang entry

ken, kent know, known
kittles up strengthens

lee falsehood

mair more
mawkin hare
mishanter accident
muckle much, a lot

naebody nobody
naethin' nothing
near han nearly
nicht night

nivver never
noo now

orraman farm labourer

peesies lapwings
pit put
puckle a few, small amount

querencia home base

richt right
roch rough
roup farm auction sale
rowe roll

sair sore
scoor diarrhoea
sharn manure
sheet shoot
siller wealth, money
skitit skidded
spik gossip
stane dyke dry stone wall
steading farm building
steen stone
stot young castrated animal
stramash fuss, bother
swark as a lop fit as a flea

teuchat lapwing
thole bear
thoomb thumb
trauchled wearied, overworked
tummelt tumbled
twa two
twalmonth year
tyauve struggle

umman woman

warsle work away, wrestle
wasna' wisnae was not
weel well
wid would
windflower wood anemone
wint want
wirk work
wither weather

yir your

1

Ingang

She could see from the kitchen window a white mist drifting across a sparse planting of young conifers on neighbouring land. Where their own parks began, a stream bordered by lush spreading junipers was too far from the house for her to hear the gush of its fall from the high hill. Deer were said to roam up there and the rare capercaillie which made sounds so harsh and distinctive that you could never mistake a 'capper' for anything else. If they had any sense, deer and capercaillie and all things with fur or feather would be somewhere under shelter on this November day specified for the move to Bithnie. It began to rain, a heavy drizzle which looked as if it meant business, but that did not matter – the animals were to be kept under cover for their first night in the new place.

The buildings were large but it was clear to Charlotte that comparing them with John's super construction at Burnside was a road to nowhere: the decision to move had been well and truly thought out, the smallest detail given consideration. They had gone for doubled acreage in a less harsh situation and buildings could be modernised: at least this old, old steading tucked cosily into the brae side could not be accused of 'stickin' oot like a sair thoomb'. She stifled any thought of changes; the new overdraft, their first ever from 'the Banker', was also large. A farm overdraft was the same as a mortgage in ordinary life but it felt different.

The farmhouse, unoccupied for a year or more, had a bleak, cold feel to it. Electric heaters of early design were not making much impact. The Aga on order would make a difference, though it was to be more expensive than the one bought for Burnside, a luxury even then. Looking round the kitchen she imagined it painted up a bit and warm, with the little white dresser in place and a decent rug, a few of their pictures... It was funny, but with a farm all normal things took second place, your house had furniture dumped in various rooms with boxes stacked high waiting to be unpacked, unlike the steading which was completely in order, everything neatly stowed under a roof which John had crawled over checking for loose slates. Hay, straw, concentrates, safe and dry; machinery ready for action. For Bithnie farm to be in business it lacked only the herd. She could picture cows staggering inside after the trauma of the floats, the way they would relish hay and concentrates laid out, and gradually settle. She and John and all involved could then say Amen.

There was a bit of a worry because the entrance to the farm was difficult, just past a bend on the road where traffic hurtled along at a rate of knots, particularly cars with skis on top headed for the slopes or coming back from them. Immediately after the bend you had to veer to the wrong side to get a turn into the rough lane leading to their bridge – a canny structure of iron with wooden sleepers, in fact a Bailey bridge crossing the River Don. In recent weeks every trip to Bithnie had included transfers of hay or straw or stores and when it was her turn John suggested not doing the suicidal loop to the right but carrying on until after a few minutes there was a piece of waste land where she could make an easy turn and thereafter a straightforward signalled right into their lane. To his surprise she had taken this easy way out. Now it was the great floats full of their precious animals to worry about. Could they do the same or would the drivers say 'Nae bother John!' and have a go? When John was arranging for the move a man in the office said, 'Is yon briggie safe then?' and John, tempting providence a little, answered, 'Tell them to wear lifebelts!' Whenever anything large or small did cross the bridge there was a clatter of wooden planks taking the strain. In the childhood story of The Three Billy Goats Gruff there is constant repetition of a phrase – 'Tric-trac, tric-trac over the rickety bridge' – and that was the Bithnie Bridge noise exactly.

No sound from the bridge but the throb of an engine and, beyond the stream, opening a farm gate for his red Land Rover was a postie who would have to be told that under the new ownership right of way was closed, as legally written into the deeds. She hoped it would be a postie she knew, perhaps the one who used strange Doric words when he spoke and liked to explain them and get her to attempt a pronunciation. She could not be faulted on 'Twas a braw bricht meenlicht nicht' but that was unsuitable. More aptly, 'Tis dreich the day!' might soften the approach if it was worth troubling. In the event the postie was a complete stranger, accepting easily what she said about the cancelled route, but she sensed curiosity having met this many times before. It was the old, old yarn about the chap frae Lunnon, 'Hid a gey fancy life and gied it up te ferm at the back o' beyont ... een wi' a muckle o'siller an' needin' his heid examin't...' Ironic one could say. Postie drove off down the farm road which needed a fair amount of siller spent on repairs and was unlikely to get any for a long time.

She looked at her watch and tried to visualise what was going on at the other farm. If the floats were on time it would be easy to load the young stock because they were already housed after the weaning. Easy only in theory: in reality anything could happen. Released from their known place the animals could be what the pundits called 'heich heidit' and go every which-way other than where you wanted, up a steep ramp into a float. If you managed to get a batch of six or seven inside the float, you then had to leap in to gate them off before the next lot were loaded, their separation essential for safe travel. The most frustrating thing on earth was if the first few walked in nicely and then a follower took fright, emptying the float at the speed of light. Everything was more difficult after such panic.

Say the young stock was loaded and the floats moved further along the close, then the herd could be brought down from the hill. They had been kept there for the night with no access to pasture but there was tasty 'natural' grass among the whins and plenty of shelter: it was a favourite place. John would make sure the floats had straw to cover the strangeness of the high metal ramps and give better foothold. The next step would be to take a plastic bucket with a few cattle nuts inside, shake it and call out 'LU-U-CY!' ... and Lucy would come and bring the others with her. If you wanted the herd for anything that was the way of it. When it was anything disagreeable like a blood test or injections, you knew you were a traitor, a betrayer of Lucy, epitome of all the virtues, model cow.

The steep ramps into the floats made loading difficult: the men would need a lot of patience before the whole herd was safely tucked away. So much depended on the nature of man and beast: John would have no sticks or switches used and soft words and quiet ways could work wonders. But there were cows like Gertie whose one residual horn kept her in poll position and commanded untold respect, and there was Irene who was very, very nervous and in the past had been a 'dyke-lowper' and some others...

Charlotte had food ready for the men and the kettle had boiled more than once. One of the many boxes of books was almost emptied when it came, the 'tric-trac, tric-trac'. She put on a waterproof and went out.

2

Mishanter

Five-thirty in the morning and John Grey was snoring persistently enough to wake Charlotte, who had been dreaming not of the farmhouse left the previous day but of the dearly loved house in England, sold to help them start the new life. In the dream she was at the window of an attic room looking down at smooth lawns and hawthorn trees all in blossom, drifts of delicate, curiously muted colour beneath each one. A pond glistening in the background was arrowed where water-hens had darted across. Marshland with a hint of sunrise on reeds and mudflats waited for a tide, and everywhere birds were wakening to the day. It was infinitely beautiful and affected her deeply. Time had a slower beat: she was aware of each long moment and the simplicity of all things until, to her surprise and sadness, a thick mist obliterated trees, flowers and the pale fallen petals. She could no longer see the marshes and the wide sky or hear the sound of any bird. She knew that something had been lost and she had to find out...

The bedroom at Bithnie had a sloped ceiling like the attic in the dream but the walls were not white, had wallpaper with roses. In bud, in full flower and overblown, quite unfaded by clear light, were roses to wake up to for a long time to come. Charlotte resolved to ignore their roistering, to dismiss them from her thinking rather than learn to love them. In effect they would go on the hit list but without priority. She snuggled under the duvet trying to make sense of her dream. How strange on their first night in a new home to dream of Wellhouse. Uprooting from there had been painful yet necessary to prove, if only to themselves, they were not people saying 'I always wanted to...', or 'If only...' but were willing to try something, facing the consequences if it failed. In the dream, why did the lovely garden dissolve with something missing that she must find?

She saw John move and could not resist telling him at length. Not fully awake he tried to understand. 'Sort of Bo-Peep...' he yawned, '...but lost cows!'

A perfunctory wash before checking the animals, breakfast coming later if all was well – a good deal later if there was trouble, and one never knew. At first sight they had been surprised that the house was not fenced off from the road the cows would take, going to and from the steading: it seemed that rolls of wire netting stacked under a window were used as a barrier. John planned a sturdy wall to enclose a small garden with a decent path, improving things for man and beast. With winter just around the corner the wall had high priority; he drew the line at Gertie having a go at the kitchen window and soon there would be a bull: Charlotte would prefer him kept away from the door.

As they splashed through puddles deep enough to annoy, John was aware of heavy loops of electric cable slapping in a desultory way against pebbledash on the old stones. It was a first priority to get the supply underground and this he would do, leaving everything else to Charlotte. Jack of all trades he had become without a doubt, and there was a certain satisfaction to that. Late last night the cows had been quiet, settled in deep straw, maybe as worn out as himself. The true picture would emerge now and anxiety quickened his steps. He remembered Charlotte dreaming of the old house: this move had to be successful for both their sakes.

He was relieved to find things still quiet, cudding cows, one or two foraging for hay, all becoming aware of him and he made reassuring noises. He saw a flicker of amusement on Charlotte's face and knew she was thinking he never spoke so sweetly to her or called her 'my dove'. They set to work replenishing makeshift troughs he had rounded up because the ones used before were now out of reach. Very different from his Atcost building, this one functioned better with a great depth of muck left in the court – all very well if the muck were dry, but he could not stand the thought of cows staggering belly-deep through mire, which must have happened over the long winter months. Again he had plans but in the meantime an expensive clearing operation gave a better start. A Ben Nevis of good muck towered at the side of the building ready for use later on. Charlotte had been thinking the same. 'I'm glad you got it done. It will be easier for us in the long run,' she said.

At Burnside they had come across Wullie, a big strong lad who tackled the muck without roll bar or cab on his sturdy little Ferguson tractor. This was risky and probably illegal, but he was cheerfully unconcerned. Neither did he grumble at the monotony of the job: 'I jis' warsle awa' till aa's deen,' he said. 'Nae bother!' He was happy 'amang the muck' and would have eaten a packed lunch there had Charlotte not brought him to eat with them. Not really fussy about washing, he obeyed when Charlotte pointed him towards the bathroom. They learned about Wullie's nights out and how he ended up in a ditch or through a hedge on the way home. Once he turned the car completely over but walked away unharmed. After any crash he turned up for work smiling as ever, the odd plaster on his forehead. 'Ye'll niver guess!...' he would say.

After attending to the cows, John saw to the young stock while Charlotte went off to feed geese housed in a shed which John intended to demolish. It was not the only eyesore on his list: in front of the farm cottage two decrepit cars had to be removed somehow. If you had a tidy mind it was hard to imagine people leaving such junk, but for some time the farm had been owned by the

Forestry Commission who rented out the arable land. It had been nobody's business to clear things up. Until now.

Out from the shed came the grey gander, wary, ready to push out his chest and fly at her if need be. His three dames, a step or two behind, blinked their eyes and made soft, anxious little noises. At the sight of an iron bowl brought from Burnside these noises rose to a joyful shriek and with a flapping of wings they rushed to settle round it as usual, yellow beaks dipped avidly into the paler corn. Given water, they would lean into it, dab fiercely at the bottom of the bucket, then throw a little over the head before a slow and graceful lift and a long stretch at the luxury of swallowing. It was nice to watch geese. They were to go into the back garden for the day and return to the shed before dark to be safe from the foxes which were likely to roam on Bithnie Hill as well as the deer and capercaillie of report. A routine would evolve, the geese would soon get their bearings. Cows, geese and us, we all have to do that, she thought.

There had been a polite fiction that the Aga ordered would be installed before they moved into the house. Until it was delivered there was the challenge of a cooker with two burners slow to heat and others which did not heat at all, not to speak of an oven thick with evidence of long forgotten meals. So preparing breakfast was a tardy business and it was fortunate that John was late to come in. He ate hugely as always, yet she saw he was bothered about something. As he buttered a second piece of toast she asked what was wrong.

'I'm not sure,' he said. 'One of the stots, number seven, seemed to me he was limping.'

The vet leaned on the rails above the cattle court and stared at the young bullocks munching at piled hay. All in good nick, cross-bred Aberdeen Angus, pushy, bright-eyed, shiny-coated, nothing wrong there; it was the one at the back and he hadn't much doubt. He sighed. He had been on the way home when the message came to call at Bithnie, a very definite request for him personally. His wife had sounded vexed because they had folks coming for dinner and she wanted him home early, out of working clothes and sweet-smelling, ready to hand round drinks and pretend he encountered only better-class animals in the most immaculate of situations, and never,

never got shat upon. However, she had relayed the specific instruction not to send the new man. A little bird must have told John Grey... To be honest the new chap wasn't to his own liking, but he needed help. If only the man fitted in a bit better, talked less and didn't wear those damned bow-ties. Or maybe his farmers were so used to a rough bugger like himself the contrast un-settled them. He turned to the man at his side: 'There's no doubt. A break at the bottom of the leg there. You shot a robin lately?'

He could have kicked himself because this farmer had no need of jokes.

'You're telling me there's nothing, no way...?'

'Well, usually folks send 'em down the road but ... let's get him out of there and I'll have a closer look.'

It was not easy. The clang of a heavy gate and a strange body among them sent a surge of panic rippling through the whole lot. A second gate to open and close, a short passage sloping to the back of the steading and a narrow doorway which the stot did not like, before they reached the haven of a small square place which had been a store for turnips. John spread a thick layer of straw over the concreted floor and waited.

The beast would not touch the hay offered to him. Head well down. A creature of the herd alone for almost the first time in his life, every trembling muscle spoke of defeat.

'An alternative to sending him off: I give him a shot and plaster him, but only with help from you. It will take some doing. I never like putting beasts right out, too many things to go wrong. It all depends on whether you can hold him down. He looks a tough boy. What do you think?'

There was no hesitation, 'I'll hold him!'

To condemn a perfectly healthy animal for so simple a thing as a broken bone was unthinkable.

'Then we'll leave him for a wee while, let him settle. I've got all I need in the back of the Wagen.'

Ample room there was, in his new vehicle. It had cost an arm and a leg but was the perfect answer to whatever winter might throw at him and he certainly knew all about that. With a start he remembered the dinner party.

'And if I may call my wife and, er, tell her I'll be delayed.'

He would be brief and take the flak later. He hoped there would be a cup of something for him now. It was going to be a tricky do.

The bullock was already down for them, the injured foot uppermost on the straw.

'On you go then. We may be lucky!'

No. Not lucky. Not John! A violent lift of all fourteen stones of him, and a great thud when his head met the wall. He saw blinding lights and was unclear about many things, except that his head was becoming a turnip and he wanted to laugh at how apt that was in a turnip shed ... and his neck seemed compressed down into his chest and there was something wet...

After a while he saw a weatherbeaten face quite close. 'You OK lad? Good! Hop back on then!'

In a dream he collapsed over the writhing animal, spreading himself, doing all but suffocate it, but this time with effect. Another terrible heave when the foot was straightened but Batman was not flying again. With less clamour in his head he could tell he was lucky to get the boss vet, the other prissy sod wouldn't have coped. Deft, this old boy, slapping the plaster on. God knows what sort of a bill, but worth it, better than the beast sent down the road.

'All done! Arise, Lazarus! Steady as you go now! Watch the peg-leg!'

John placed hay where the stot could reach it and shut the door on him. He stood while the vet loaded his stuff into the back of the Mercedes G-Wagen, then after a moment went back to put his head under the steading tap. He didn't want Charlotte to get a shock.

'You'll take a dram?' he called, shaking icy water from his turnip head.

3

Dool

John slept restlessly, groaning when now and again his sore head touched sheet or pillow. Awake, Charlotte switched on a bed-side lamp to find the swelling exposed and ugly, witch-hazel from the loose dressing had soaked into the pillow. Holding her breath she managed to replace it without waking him. She also moved the alarm clock to her own side of the bed.

Waking as light illumined the rosy wall, John cursed at the unnatural feel of his head and more loudly when he saw the time: you could never recoup lost hours. Scrambling into his clothes he got downstairs, at each step aware of a pendulum swing in his head and a painful stiffness in his neck. Flushed, and less than neat but smiling, Charlotte was filling the kettle.

'Nae bother!' she said attempting the Doric, 'aa's deen!' In fact at one time she had almost lost it. Feeding with hay had gone reasonably well but cattle nuts were a nightmare for a lone body. Clamped tight between jostling beasts it had been vital to get her hands flat on their warm backs and push upwards, push hard before her ribs gave way. Feet leaving the ground she had been carried along, hardly able to get breath. Not funny at all. She would keep silent about that until the turnip head was normal. Meantime, how lovely it was to sit and how good the bacon tasted, and John looked a bit better.

The vet's white G-Wagen nosed its way up the rough road leading to Bithnie on a mission to check the stot and also John Grey. He felt pretty certain the animal would be all right but, as his wife pointed out more than once, he tended to have a cavalier attitude when immersed in a job of work, did not care about anything or anyone else and simply forgot about other people's feelings. Anyway, today he could judge and suggest a doctor if the man looked dodgy. Last night he had been given a warmed-up main course while the others drank coffee and guzzled his brandy in the next room. His wife said very little until the guests were away. Now he saw John Grey walk to meet him.

'No ill-effects then? Bloody but unbowed eh?' he asked, relief making him jaunty.

'Beautiful as always,' John answered on cue, 'like the queen.'

That expression, from his days in the Service, always irritated Charlotte for some reason and he was glad she wasn't there to hear him resurrect it.

'Come and take a look at peg-leg,' he offered.

Number seven had plenty of hay, a full tank of water and deep straw for a bed. Head up and bright of eye he was firmly on his feet, the whiteness of the plastered leg only a little less pristine. Eagerly he sniffed at the hand outstretched.

'See? He does not bear malice! What did the poet say? "I think I could turn and live with animals, they are so placid..." Excepting yesterday of course! "I stand and look at them, long and long..." Good that, eh? I've always liked that!'

'Yes. You think of some long-haired chap, maybe brought up on a farm, hasn't seen a cow for years but remembers, gets it exactly right. Looking at cows... We spend hours just looking, Charlotte and me.'

They exchanged wry smiles. After the blood and sweat of the previous day it was pleasant to stand and talk about a poet.

While number seven was getting the treatment and John suffering the consequences of it, the cows had explored the small paddock below the house but in reality there was nothing for them to eat, the grass entirely spent. By the time the vet had driven off and John had explained about his contact with the wall, there was a mute cluster of bodies at the gate. All were anxious for food and the shelter of the steading. Shelter. 'Bield' was the old Scots word and in a Scottish winter both man and beast would have need of it.

On their third day, after the morning feed, Charlotte had opened a gate at the far end of the paddock giving access to another park. Because cows like to spread widely over their grazing and are curious, one of them pushed against a gate in this new field, a wooden one quite easy to knock down to give them all access to the wood.

Fresh woods? Old, old oaks, beeches, elms, rowans and gean trees. A lovely place. People had mentioned the woodland at Bithnie, acres of it bordering the River Don.

'Gey fine for yir beese in coorse wither.' This particular part of the woodland figured on John's work list: a wall to rebuild; posts and piky wire, and fallen branches to clear. He had also noted NEW GATE and queried, METAL?

When the next feed was due and no cows gathered pushing at the paddock gate, John and Charlotte went to look for them and found all placid, undamaged by any hazards, exploring under the trees for what there was of 'natural' grass.

Here again was the call, 'LU-CY, LU-U-CY!' and of course she came, the model cow, the rest following. Except one at the bottom of the wood.

'I'll go and get started. You fetch her. I think it's Buttercup.' John gave Lucy's tail-head an affectionate scratch as she passed. Charlotte could hear him talking to his 'girls' as he walked back but she had the easier job with only one to see to. She picked her way towards the last cow – Buttercup it was. She felt irritated when instead of walking towards her the beast slowly moved as if to escape.

But then she was easily turned in the right direction and they made progress, but it was slow, as if the cow wanted to stay where she was and not follow the herd. Unusual that. 'Oh do come on lassie' met little response and because the light was going Charlotte gave a more urgent, 'Come on, come on girl!' and a light slap across the rump. Buttercup was a dark red cow with a white face; this she turned slowly to Charlotte with eyes that did not seem to see and then she sank to the long grass to lie shuddering there. Within seconds the movement stopped.

4

Chokit

'Hypomagnesaemia: a condition in which there is too little magnesium in the bloodstream can be experienced when a herd is turned out onto lush spring grass.' The book also said it could occur in late autumn or winter, sometimes after a snowfall or a cold, wet spell. Most people knew it as 'the staggers'.

It was a puzzle trying to get enough magnesium into the cows. They had blocks with supplements added to improve the taste, and these were very expensive. Bossy types like Gertie who used the horn to stake her claim to anything were ever guzzling at them, and cows lower in the 'bunt' or order of importance never got near. John placed containers of magnesium powder both outside and in the courts; the outside ones were made useless when it rained, the inside ones were up-ended or 'shat' upon. It needed a rethink at Bithnie. The vet suggested the move from one farm to another could have a lot to do with Buttercup's demise, perhaps tipped her over the edge. At another time the symptoms might have been seen and remedies taken. Meanwhile, watch the others... John did not need telling.

Both John and Charlotte had been stunned by the death. Somehow through crises of various kinds they had kept the original herd intact. This was their first loss of a cow and irrationally they blamed themselves.

'There's naethin' for't bit te mak the best o'a bad job,' said Wullie. 'Ye've jis' te thole it when een o'the buggers dees on ye.'

Of course he was right, but with number seven a near-miss and now Buttercup, it had not been a good start at the new farm. As always there were practical problems: a body on a rough track inaccessible by tractor had to be roped and dragged to the nearest gate, uplifted and brought back by tractor to await the knacker-man. A sweaty desperate job, but the two of them managed it. Never had the old life seemed so desirable, the new one so alien, but they did not put it into words. John saw a white, set face and knew his own must have the same look. It was an awful business.

As a precaution the vet supplied bottles of magnesium and a flutter valve attached to rubber tubing with a stout needle at its end. He gave precise instructions: if the symptoms were evident, secure the cow behind a gate; replace the bottle cap with the flutter valve and insert the needle beneath the skin of her neck, taking great care not to penetrate muscle. Stand on a rung of the gate holding the bottle high to allow the magnesium to drip steadily into the cow. If the cow is off her feet, make sure the bottle is held as high as possible. In extreme cases two bottles may be needed.

Where to keep this vital magnesium? Charlotte had been shattered by the thought of other cows in urgent need of treatment, the whole herd requiring bottles and bottles of the stuff.

'Could we have it with us all the time? Say in a large handbag?'

'A haaandbag?' John said, like Lady Bracknell, but neither felt like smiling. Carrying the stuff around all the time was impractical yet it had to be kept at the ready, where they could uplift quickly. They settled for a strong plastic bag with handles and placed it on a coathook just inside the back door. An unmistakable dark green, it bore the name 'Harrods'.

On the concreted floor of the former dairy in Bithnie farmhouse stood only the freezer and a washing machine as yet unplumbed. They visualised the place with another sink and cupboards where veterinary supplies and anything to do with the animals could be separated from household and normal kitchen use. When the Aga arrived they hoped its warmth would percolate from the main kitchen to dispel the dampness here, as in other rooms. A telephone call had come from Aberdeen.

'Mrs Grey? I am pleased to tell you your Aga has been despatched to us and will arrive any day.'

41

So the old cooker with the duff burners could be taken away to wherever such things go. *Deo gratias.*

Cheered by this news, Charlotte took the key and walked over to the cottage. When they looked round the farm in the summer everything was tentative, the small cottar house a lesser detail. Other thoughts occupied them: whether they could cope with a much larger farm, what sum of money would be needed for a successful bid, and still more important, did they really want to leave Burnside? Now here they were at Bithnie, the massive upheaval completed and other troubles dealt with. She was looking forward to things being more normal. In the summer they could ask friends to stay in the cottage. Quite unaffected by the workings of the farm, people could get up late, laze about, come across to the house for meals cooked beautifully in the Aga. It was pleasant to think of all that.

She turned before putting the large old-fashioned key into the lock, remembering the surprise of a magnificent view of clustering small houses, farms, gently undulating land stretching to distant hills; the Howe of Alford under a wide blue sky. Today was cold and raw with nothing to see under clouds heavy with rain; parks shown in the sale prospectus glowing with corn were hazed in mist from the river. You had to know 'the bonny days' would come again.

The door opened onto a porch of tongued and grooved wood, its paint faded and flaking, the floor concreted. Beneath the window a wide shelf was convenient for household things or plants needing plenty of light. A further door opened into a short passage leading on the left to a living room and tiny kitchen. On the right was a twisting staircase, a bathroom with plain white fittings, and a sitting room. As expected the bedrooms had rosy wallpaper and sloping ceilings. Over all was the familiar smell of soot and damp. The two fireplaces were decent enough and a good fire in each would work wonders. Locking up again Charlotte saw among weeds by the door a tarnished brass plate, the name almost worn away. She pictured the house neat and tidy with smart paint and a garden bright with flowers. Was it like that a very long time ago, the doorplate gleaming, buffed up daily by a proud wifie?

Probably built at the same time as the steading, the little house was also tucked cosily into the brae: they had known a thing or two about shelter in the old days. She had time to climb the slope where on their first visit she had noticed wild roses, but after a few steps she was thunderstruck. She saw bottles – bottles, cans, boxes, any kind of rubbish, lumber, trash, junk from a lifetime stacked and spilling over a little path behind the house. The mind boggled. What did you do? Chuck everything out of the windows? Say to a child, 'Pop this outside for me, anywhere you like!' She stared, and after a moment, feeling a need for roses, began the steep climb up the brae.

At the top she did find bare and straggling bushes which would have a brief June glory. 'You ain't seen nuthin' yet' applied to the hole, the large, deep hole containing oil drums and tyres, troughs, feeders, ploughs and harrows; enormous heaps of rusty, disintegrating farm stuff. Tilted into the rose bushes like a crown was another old banger.

Charlotte walked back to the house in a daze. How to break the news to John? They had enough on without this labour of Hercules. She remembered her fantasy about the proud wifie and had to smile because in the debris there was no sign of little stripey tins marked 'Brasso'.

5

Dunt

For the Bithnie kitchen they had chosen a solid fuel cooker after the experience at Burnside when winter snow brought down electricity cables, putting the pump out of action which controlled an oil-fired one. Anthracite and phurnacite in hundred-weight bags had to be accommodated in a decrepit shed listed for demolition.

'Funny how we keep using the old eyesores!' John said. 'At this rate it won't be long before we start a bottle mountain!' In the event, a pile of ashes arose ready for when there was ice to contend with.

In the steading, work always warmed them and little by little they stripped off coats, sweaters or cardigans. Warmth in the house made a tremendous difference to the number of necessary layers and Charlotte's legwarmers were put away for the time being. Good food played a part, soups and casseroles fuelling energy for tackling items on

John's list in the brief time before the second feed and early nightfall.

The new owners at Burnside showed great concern about the injured stot and the loss of the cow. The introduction to this family interested in buying a farm took place one afternoon when Charlotte had answered a tap at the door, imagining it was the usual summons from the grey gander greedy for extra rations.

'Oh hello there!' she gestured with the slice of bread, 'I thought you were a goose!'

'I am!' Margaret smiled. 'Very often!'

She had liked the farm and returned to Aberdeen to tell her husband all about it and afterwards wrote to Charlotte:

Dear Mrs Grey,
I felt I must write a note and say how much I enjoyed meeting you both and also to say 'thank you' for showing me round in such an enjoyable and honest manner. It was of course a bonus to meet a 'southerner' and another bonus to see such well cared for stock. Whatever comes of this (the possibilities of which are being looked into) I hope we shall meet again.
Sincerely
Margaret (the Goose)

That was the beginning and it continued with great goodwill on both sides. Their son, who came home from Australia to run the farm, was as charming and enthusiastic as his parents, and keen to rear good animals on Burnside. Some time later on the way to visit John and Charlotte at Bithnie he called at the garage in Alford.

'I've jis' had yir father in,' said Mr Smith. 'Nae ten minutes sin!'

Dugald had looked puzzled because his father was playing golf, miles away. Then the penny dropped: both of them bearded, new to Donside, he and John had been linked, a Scottish version of 'They all look the same!'

'Naah!' John shook his head at the bronzed and smiling young man, 'They wouldn't think you were my son, not good-looking enough.'

'Tell Dugald about the barber, John.'

It was like a wife to remind him. On a rare visit to Aberdeen for farm supplies, he had gone into a rather faded little shop in Bucksburn, being unwilling to pay ransom money in a smarter town 'salon'. He had been uncomfortable with hair grown longer than at any time in his whole life, 'like a blasted pop star', but grudged any time away from the

47

farm. He was pleased with his new short back and sides and rather taken aback when the barber, sweeping up a tidy pile, volunteered: 'A wid like fine te see ye mair'n eence in a twal-month ye ken'...Ye're aa' the same frae the bluidy oil-rigs!' and in a voice devoid of hope as John closed the shop door, 'See ye nex' yeer!'

After cups of tea they took Dugald to see the cattle. As the vet and the poet said, you could stand and look at them long and long and number seven was a star. They peered over the half-door of the turnip shed where, looking a little bit dejected, he was nosing at the hay-rack.

'I think he is fed-up in there,' said Charlotte. 'Lonely on his own, and he could do with some exercise.'

The remedy was easy. Dugald helped them block off each end of the passage at the back of the court. This walkway gave access to the original troughs neither cows nor young stock could reach, but number seven would be able to lean over, touch uplifted noses, 'speak' to other animals and in a limited sort of way become part of the family again. Pleased with their efforts, the only thing remaining was to see the effect when John unbolted the door.

It was nil. No effect whatsoever. Number seven had decided to have a rest. On his bed, peacefully cudding, he lifted a mild eye at their appearance in his querencia and truth to tell did not look even slightly lonely.

'Ah well,' said John. 'I suppose I'll be the one getting the exercise, climbing over all the bloody gates!'

Eventually they got their reward. When the cows came back to feed, number seven was out, hobbling on three good legs and a peg, back and forth, happily greeting his mates in the court. They put out hay for him and he settled to eat, after a while lifting his tail to produce a healthy splatter. 'By the way,' John was all innocence. 'I forgot to mention that the one who was concerned about his civil liberties has to deal with the sharn!'

All was going well, the pattern more or less the same as in the winter months at Burnside. Cows went off daily after the first feed and in turn the parks were opened up for them to find an elusive bite. By half-past three in the afternoon they were clustering round the gate nearest the steading. After the morning feed was finished John and Charlotte got the next one ready: hay in the racks, mineral powder, beet nuts or barley in containers, the court strawed out and water troughs checked. The court gate was then firmly bolted even though the gate on the brae had been shut after the last cow. That sort of thing came with experience: it was devastating to find carefully prepared and rationed food all gone because one clever cow and a few buddies had found a way...

Number seven complicated things of course: all expensive concentrates had to be locked away and hay bales placed out of his reach. He got more than his share of attention, a star turn who astonished visitors at the speed he could muster when beet nuts were around and the smell reached him.

'Like the Aga Khan,' John explained, 'he is worth his weight in gold. What with the bill for his leg and Charlotte indulging his every whim, I am likely to end up on Union Street. Think of it! Me outside British Home Stores with a placard saying BANKRUPTED BY ABERDEEN ANGUS.'

'By a very *healthy* Aberdeen Angus,' reminded Charlotte, who did spend a fair amount of time with bucket and shovel. Her care for number seven evoked the nursery rhyme, 'Mary had a Little Lamb' but after a time she became unsure who was Mary.

The weather was turning colder, with sharp frosts at night. Water for the farm was described in the prospectus as 'plentiful own water supply': mains water was not available. This was usual for most farms and had not concerned them, but the Bithnie water certainly had a long way to travel by rather inefficient means. Here, as at their other farm, details handed over about water supply or drainage were sketchy to say the least; only by trial and error did the facts become known. Just below Forestry planting, way up on Bithnie Hill they found a small tank made of cemented concrete blocks into which water from the hill collected. A short pipe led from this first tank into a bigger one, also of concrete blocks. From the second tank, pipes led to troughs on the braes and to a large metal tank behind the cottar house, branching off there, and also down the brae to the steading and eventually the house. This water, which certainly passed no tests or safety standards, was somehow pure and sweet to the taste.

However, the long and tortuous journey of more than a mile from pipe to tap increased the chances of things going wrong and over the weeks they did. More than once stones blocked the system and the piping between tanks one and two had to be replaced. Cows damaged the vital ballcocks in the troughs and bawled for the precious water coursing down the brae. It does not need saying that failure surprised them at the worst moments when they were dealing with some crisis in the court or were exhausted by heavy work. Inevitably this happened in bad weather.

A bag of tools is heavier, the brae steeper, with an icy wind against you. Real rain, not gentle, stings and blinds, penetrates and soaks to the shivering skin. In heavy snow, each plunged foot is hard to get back: The brae, so easy in the bonny days, is Everest with no summit. But the trek is made because cows must have water. Nothing more clearly points to the difference between farming and ordinary life. Say your water supply is cut off in the town, you drink bottled water, rub yourself with cologne if you are fussy, and wait. A cow drinks copiously, her need so great that she can only tell you by bawling loud and long; she simply cannot do without it. Complaining maybe into the shrieking winds, you climb to clear the blockage. On the way back you have the goal of a warm kitchen and a drop of the other kind of water Scots know about and call the water of life.

Apart from any kind of drouth the fates which govern removals had not quite finished with John. One day in very icy conditions, anxious to keep the cattle inside for safety, he went to shut the gate as soon as the last cow entered the court. The gate was wide and extremely strong, made to resist a good deal of pressure from weighty bodies. Molly, the last in, was probably their most powerful animal but fairly amenable. Maybe John was a little hasty clanging the gate behind her. Startled, she kicked it back ... a great shudder and blinding lights once more for John as a thick rounded bar crashed into his face.

Managing somehow to shoot the bolt across, John accused: 'My God, Molly! Molly, you bastard cow! You've ... you've broken my bloody nose!'

And truly it was very, very bloody.

Again there was sympathy from the Burnside family. Doctor W. enquired if John would manage to get the operation.

'An operation?' John's face, enhanced by colourful black eyes and a swollen nose, showed bewilderment. 'What for?'

The answer 'For cosmetic reasons' was not in his understanding.

'No!' he said. 'It doesn't matter when you've got a beautiful soul like mine.'

6

Gallop

Christmas cards were to be special ones made from photographs with captions such as HOME IS THE HUNTER, showing John carrying a gun over a snow-deep hill, and AS I WALK'D THROUGH THE WILDERNESS OF THIS WORLD, with Charlotte the pilgrim in an expanse of shining white. Others, when the snow had gone, were of mothers and calves with a dazzle of gorse behind them. Charlotte guessed the snow pictures might evoke shudders but the others were sure to generate 'oohs' and 'aahs': whatever people thought of their venture, the images were charming. She did not include any of Gertie to spoil the illusion.

Although Charlotte liked writing and thinking of old friends, there was the worry of John managing the feeds and steading work on his own. In reality only correspondence with the Department of Agriculture and Fisheries mattered to John. Left to him no Hunter, no Pilgrim, no sweet calves and mums would send regards.

'I'm full of goodwill,' he insisted, 'absolutely brimming over! Watch me on Christmas Day raising my glass to absent friends as often as you like!' So Charlotte got on with it. Contrasted with the demands of a normal day, sitting at a desk was rest and refreshment: with coffee to hand and a growing pile of completed cards she was more than content.

'We make a good pair,' she said. 'You full of goodwill and me a sybarite, a "lady wife" at last. You can raise a glass to that as well!'

Because cows have no concept of 'holiday' such a thing did not exist for John or Charlotte. They took time to eat a fine dinner, drank the toasts, saw one or two friends, but Christmas passed quietly. North of the border New Year was the time for real celebration. People made visits to friends but acquaintances and strangers were drawn in: goodwill blanketed the Howe. On the farms routine work was rushed so the fun could begin early. Crates in Land Rover or car would hold bottles of everything you would fancy drinking and some stranger, well-advertised concoctions that you would not.

A noisy arrival on a farm close. Greetings:

'Ay Ay! Fit like?'; 'Fit's new wi ye?'; 'Happy N'Yeer!'; and inside the house, 'Ye'll tak'a dram?' You did and also offered with maybe 'twa or three' to follow and perhaps a little food. This the pattern, until at some house the hour struck and the year was truly new. More rough farm tracks and distant houses for the hardy ones; more greetings, more drams and food but never a thought of sleep or being 'tipsy in charge'. Early on the great day you come to a house where the man is just about to feed his stock: very well then, help him and afterwards breakfast on the fresh rolls you collected when greeting the baker and the bacon his wife is crisping. As well as a cup of tea, lift a glass of your spirits and the one he will offer, and before going on your way a kiss for the wifie and for both a benison – 'Look efter yersels', gweed folk's scarce!'

John and Charlotte never acquired the stamina for Hogmanay, never took part in a jolly roving party, but offered hospitality *in situ* and in between bursts got some sleep. Waiting for the midnight sounds to float across the land they looked at the beasts and were content. How true in the night hours that cows are 'so placid and self-contained' and plainly 'Not one is demented with the mania of owning things'.

Someone witnessing the fine concentration of animals eating in the Atcost building at Burnside remarked in something like awe, 'It is like being in a church!' The faults of the Bithnie steading need a kindly darkness to cover them but the beasts are the same. In response to words from John walking through the court a soft nose lifts to his hand. Quiet eyes are watchful but the comfortably-disposed bodies do not move, this night check is not the time for food. The stones of the older building take in the essences of today to hold with those that do not change – of corn, hay, animals. A glimmering dusk can hint of harvests when many hands were at work, unlike the swift economy of today's operation. The wings of a barn owl make only a whisper of sound as he leaves a high perch: there have been many owls and many quiet wings in this place.

When a wind 'kittles up', is 'snell', when a 'howd o' win' blaws', 'cauldrife' winter' is tightening a grip. A barn stacked with bales is then beyond price, like a full freezer in the house, and all the 'squirreling awa' of early months pays its dividend. At Bithnie life became harder. The steading roof had become heavy with snow and rising warmth from the animals had thawed it a little: through unseen holes it dripped to ice the concrete floor and make walking a hazard.

'Nae doot o'that,' as Wullie said. 'Aa nearhan brak mi neck fin aa skitit!'

The cows did not leave the steading so strawing out was less efficient. Their appetite increased at an alarming rate. Hay had to be kept dry and all feedstuffs protected, but shifting icy wrappers lengthens the time taken to feed. If things were especially bad, number seven had to be shut up in his turnip shed again where he banged about and snorted anger and learned that kicking with a peg leg is a non-starter. Late one day in early January the vet called, the younger vet who chatted as if he knew them well.

'Thank you no, John! I'll not have a dram because by all the saints he would kill me if I trashed the vehicle. Letting me drive his precious Wagen went agin' the grain, I can tell you. In all truth he detests it. But I'm taking every call with himself off with the flu and that vehicle is the only safe one with the roads as they are. The state of the little roads you'd never believe, though of course you live here and probably do know. Excuse me going on a bit, everybody thinks of me as a

58

blatherskite which is what I am I suppose! Thank you very much for the tea Mrs Grey. That was delightful cake too, home-made of course. Now the reason for this visit is...'

John saw his eyes taking in every detail in the room: the bright plates on the dresser, the chairs, books, their own well-worn work clothes, and the eyes did not convey the same message as the burbling words or the self-deprecating smile crumpling his mouth. He was dressed like a countryman except the clothes were band-box new and he smelled of aftershave. He had stepped carefully in his elegant boots so did not need to take them off at the door like other people. According to Wullie, 'The lassies were fair pleast wi' the new vetrinnery.' He certainly held Charlotte's attention: she was looking at the bow-tie.

The boss vet had sent a bottle of malt whisky with compliments and best wishes for the New Year. He hoped to be along shortly to remove the plaster. The messenger begged for a sight of the bullock.

'To be honest with you John, I would in all conscience have advised you otherwise but to be sure we all have our different little ways and disagreeable as it may be we are forced to bow to the inevitable sometimes.'

A moment of silent communication between husband and wife. Thank God for the old vet, because keeping his nice clothes un-sullied and telling them in a hushed tone how sorry he was, this man would have packed off number seven in a brace of shakes. As if to confirm, he frowned at the comfortable belly and peg leg disposed on a fair pile of straw and sighed.

'Well, you never know, it might turn out for the best in this case. The boss does a very fine job, as a rule.'

They made their way out into air that was freezing fast. A film of ice already silvered the road in front of the steading. Predictably the vet turned back to get a handful of straw to swish over his boots.

Later that evening the Greys braved the cold to go to the pub, rare for them but they had promised to meet friends. A roaring fire, drinks and congenial company made time pass all too quickly and then they were on the way home, John expert now at the dread hairpin bend leading to their bridge. He decided to leave the car at the cottage so as not to disturb the cattle. A gate crystalled over by frost burned to the touch. The air was wine. Everything sparkled: stones on the dykes, the whitened fields, their house and the buildings outlined by moonlight, and a sky bright with stars. Perfection.

It did not last. Round the corner softly illumined by light from the steading an apparition wavered, swallowing like a drowning man great gulps of precious air. One of the apparition's legs bore an off-white plaster cast.

'My God! He's finished if he steps out...'

Galvanised, they reached the nearest doorway in seconds.

'Go in the back and call him. I'll head him off!'

It was too late. Number seven was on the frozen concrete, bewildered as his feet slid in every direction, the plaster dragging. Unable to speak, hardly to breathe, they watched. He skated but miraculously did not fall and in his sights was the paddock with an open gate. Easily through this he was soon gathering pace down the slope to familiar ground. A tentative canter developed, became a near gallop. What heaven to go round and round, a black body hurtling across a field of white, and round again, faster, wilder. Aghast the watchers saw plaster break and bounce off, splints fly like missiles, ricochet over the grass, yards and yards of bandage unfurl as a pennant signalling to the night sky and to all the world that number seven had made a bid for freedom.

Glorious, but it had to end. He slowed and Charlotte ran to the gateway, urgently calling his name. The familiar voice registered and he came, puffing and blowing up the slope to difficulty again, feet sliding all at odds and tired legs not obedient any more. Eventually he was safely gated in and munching beet nuts he did not deserve.

The question of who failed to secure the gate against an ingenious creature avid for the great outside was unsolved but there was a prime suspect with very clean boots.

7

Freeze

'What freezings have I felt, what dark days seen...' The hill farmer when snow has been heavy has little contact with human beings other than his immediate family and everything he does is made more difficult. He will have stored food for house and farm and is likely to worry about these stores lasting out. The household will be engaged in a struggle to keep a water supply. A freeze brings amongst other troubles the enormous fatigue of having to do by hand things normally done by machinery. There is the acute misery of frozen fingers, chilblains, bad colds; animals denied their usual habit of grazing can be cussed, and yet, the air will be like wine and the unbroken white over his fields and his neighbour's fields and the far off hills will be a sight to behold, only surpassed when a rare sun gilds it or gives the glory of a sunset.

It is a harsh fact that with a rise in temperature this farmer is in no way better off. The cold winds blasting his steading may have eased, he may shed a sweater or two, but instead of precarious ice his dogged feet meet with slush and damp finds a way into his boots. Water gushes from scarred pipes and blocked drains, and bubbles mysteriously in his path: it floods his empty cottar house if not the farmhouse, which is better heated. Dark clouds roll over the skies to threaten him. Wet, muddy and dispirited, he sees no golden glow on the diminishing snow: his world is sullen, grey and mud-streaked.

Charles Murray, a poet 'weel kent' in the Howe, wrote: 'Noo that cauldrife winter's here there's a pig in ilka bed...' No pig, or ceramic hot-water bottle at Bithnie, but an electric blanket sorely needed. The freeze-up, beginning when number seven made his freedom bid, continued: day followed day of bitter winds and searing cold and each night the iron grip on the land hardened until finally, their worst fear, water did not flow from the hill. Work for John then in the steading, stretches of ancient pipes to free from insulating wadding carefully applied in the early days, and as learned at Burnside, the hair-dryer brought into action. It took a long time but at first in a trickle and then in a stronger flow water was there for the animals to take the great draughts so necessary to them. Success. The flow was kept by constant drinking during the day-time; at night there was no alternative but to leave a tap running. Deciding the correct amount of flow was a problem: too little and the nightmare was repeated, too much and precious liquid was away down the drain. In the house they had no luck, the taps were dry and that was that. Buckets and kettles taken to the steading were carried back with difficulty. Anything spilled froze into a new hazard, the chore additional to other work made more burdensome by the great freeze. They forgot what it was like to have plentiful clean clothes, showers, baths. After a meal plates and dishes were dried off with kitchen paper. Washing up in hot water became a forgotten art and perfect hygiene was attempted only so far as the animals were concerned.

It was a great blessing to have an invitation from friends in the village for a meal and baths.

'I take it they mean baths first?' said John, and Charlotte agreed it was the tactful way.

'Don't bother to bring towels,' Heather said, understanding the situation well. To soak in delicious scented water was heaven. No hurry because there were two bathrooms. Warmth, clean hair, clean clothes. Forgotten bliss! A lovely dinner, wine, good company. Excellent hosts, Stuart and Heather had surpassed themselves, the baths inspirational, a crowning touch long to be remembered. The return journey, chugging along icy roads in a Land Rover slow to warm up, did not spoil things: the Bithnie 'fermers' were renewed.

Serious worries remained: the cattle were running through rations at a rate of knots and the stock of magnesium was dangerously low. The supplier was only a few miles away, the main road passable with particular care at the hairpin bend approaching Bithnie. The problem was the angled turn his articulated vehicle had to make to get onto the bridge. John did his best to stress this point but as always the response was cheerful.

'Nae bother John, I ken the briggie weel, jis' you wait!' They did wait, and at the appointed time could hardly bear to watch him lurch almost out of control down the lane and at the end of it stop, the load teetering dangerously towards the swirling water. It required superhuman effort to back away inch by inch and try again. Perhaps there was a fraction of space between the wagon and the iron rails but it was perilously close. Did he glimpse willows leaning into the thin grasp of ice at the river bank, or the dark central flow the ice could not tame? Easy over bumps on the farm road and a wide grin for John waiting at the steading. Both knew he had sweated blood: it was not the day for a dip.

Using any vehicle over frozen snow it was best to keep to ruts made previously. It was annoying when on the farm road other people did not do the same. The Land Rover would then slide through the breaks in the ruts, and in an attempt to regain the track it would skid, slither wildly and end up in deep snow. In the early days of winter John on returning from the village finding the farm road newly blocked, managed to slide back in his own ruts to an opened gate and from there drove home through the fields. Strong winds had blown the snow through fences onto the road and piled it in deep drifts at the gateways but in the fields it was not so deep. Later John went for supplies using the John Deere tractor, by arrangement meeting a friend, John Fowler, who heaved a sack of 'tatties' into the cab, groceries from the village shop filling the remaining space. Gossiping to another customer John happened to mention that the Bithnie television was giving trouble. He did not expect what followed.

'Jis' you ging te ma dochter's, she'll gie ye the loan of een frae the shop window.'

And it was true! 'Aa'll hiv it back whenniver yeer ain gits sorted,' said that young lady.

So, a little bit cramped, with potatoes and groceries, a newspaper, a bottle of the old Macallan and a few other necessities, the television on his knees, John made a triumphant return, blessing kindness in the Howe.

When a thaw came, driving was easier,

merely a matter of coasting down a shallow stream that used to be the road, taking care to avoid the deepish holes where digging out had occurred.

8

Spate

Intermittent thawing, perhaps brilliant sunshine to lift the spirit, but always a return to below-zero temperatures which had become the norm. Then stronger sun and true thaw. Noise, a low booming growing in intensity, chilling to hear: the river in spate. Chunks of ice jostling branches broken from willows, and whole trunks swept featherlight in a fearsome volume of water. It was said of the Scottish rivers, 'River Don taks one. River Dee needs three': one drowned man to compare with three. In those days the roaring Don could have 'takken fower'...

Finally the water, no longer contained, spilled to the braes' edge, a lake for Bithnie, with gulls swooping and lifting to circle a leaden sky.

The focus changed when in house and steading the effects of the thaw had to be faced. Water everywhere. Water pouring from fractured pipes to seep into the courts, dripping from roofs, flowing over blocked drains – the result a morass and desperate effort to keep the cattle reasonably dry when supplies of straw were running out. Beside a newly-built wall a stream bubbled up and flowed across the garden to flood the former dairy. The Aga had kept the kitchen warm and given a little warmth to the dairy but not sufficient to prevent the freeze that stopped their supply. John quickly repaired holes in the piping. Jack of all trades? Yes, and Charlotte for the first time a plumber's mate! There was no chance of outside help and with so many bursts a live-in plumber was better even if his repairs had to be elementary. Jubilee clips, rubber from old tyres and polythene piping all played a part. The first count revealed fourteen bursts but more would not have surprised them. Away from the buildings any bubbling up of water entailed a great deal of hard digging but the flow had to be stopped and a repair made however often a pick had to swing before pipes were found. Such work for already tired muscles seemed to go on forever. Water springing out of the road reminded them of Malham Cove where in kinder times they had seen the source of the River Aire. Here at Bithnie, helped by the slope of the land, all aspiring tributaries flowed towards the Don.

When John attacked frozen surfaces with a pick the effect of intermittent thaw and freeze was clear. As thick as concrete slabs sold to make a path or patio and just as hard and unyielding, layer upon layer of ice showed in section, like an illustration in a book on geology.

In the steading at the back of the court were places where in former days animals had been tied for fattening, with a manger and water for each partitioned stall. Tying did not necessarily entail suffering but Charlotte hated the idea. *Autre temps, autre moeurs.* Now they did not need to supply water to these stalls, enabling John to simplify the system of pipes by replacing old ones, damaged or not, with polythene piping: when insulated this might freeze but would not burst. He blessed the day he purchased great rolls of the stuff, worth its weight in gold now.

Further afield there was more to do. At the very highest point of their land, ice had formed oddly-shaped boulders diverting the flow of water so that only a little went into the tank and the rest was wasted. Hacking away at these blocks returned the supply to normal. There was more waste on the high braes: in several places mini-cascades streaked greying turf left by the vanishing snow. Polythene pipe once more, to replace copper which had split, the water troughs made ready for whenever cattle could graze again.

A black cat in Bithnie farmhouse was making his way to the basket at the side of the Aga, the best billet he felt entitled to as the youngest of Charlotte's three. It had to be said that he was a fighter unlikely to be challenged for the warmest spot by either Grey Boy or the misnamed Tiger, who had not yet turned up for his evening meal. Charlotte looked through the window at sleety snow driving across a darkening sky and sighed: it was impossible not to feel downhearted about more snow. The winter had been bad enough already, how long would this stuff last? Was it another long freeze or a mere blip before any sign of spring? She peered out again and saw Tiger, snow-spiked like a hedgehog, padding for home. She was ready at the door with a towel, scooping him up to dry and rub at his soft fur. Tiger, somehow unable to make use of the fact that he was the biggest cat, was treated with disdain by the beautiful Grey Boy but was Blackie's target and victim. Gentle and long-suffering, like a cow far down in the order of the bunt, he needed protection.

'There you are, Tiger-Muffin.' Charlotte dropped a kiss onto a cold nose and fetched food to set before him. 'No you don't Blackie!' she growled at the black cat who was willing to appropriate a second supper. Blackie went back to the Aga, planning to try again when the woman's back was turned. A nervous Tiger knew this and so did Charlotte, who stood on guard until the plate was cleared.

Next for feeding, John and herself. A casserole had slowly cooked whilst they were at work doling out rations, strawing the courts, tidying generally and leaving things ready for morning. Nowadays the chores were done with more and more concern about supplies. Hay, straw and the so-expensive concentrates seemed to vanish at an alarming rate.

John arrived from cleaning away the grime of the day. He was scrubbed and healthy-looking but by no means smart in clothes that had seen better days. A hole at the elbow of his sweater would get bigger, as Charlotte was unlikely to manage a 'stitch in time'.

Reading fashion items from any newspaper suggested that their increasingly shabby clothes might come under the heading 'distressed' rather than disreputable.

John was hungry and tucked into the casserole with relish. 'Good, that!' he said and helped himself to more.

'There is a pudding.' Charlotte lifted it from the oven. 'Draw the curtains first John, and shut that lot out!' She felt the need for warmth and comfort after a day made harder by the latest weather and the bright kitchen was a pleasant place.

'Oh my God, Charlotte, look out there!'

John was into his coat and away, Charlotte quick to follow. He had seen a cow in the steading's wide doorway, Molly he thought, and above her a broken cable slapped at the wall, sparking as it was blown against a metal strapping on the door frame. With jaws rolling as always after an intake of food, the cow was watching the blowing snow, placid, mild-eyed, oblivious of the spluttering coil. Changing the overhead cable was a priority on John's list but the fracture now meant a temporary repair he could well have done without.

Very quietly he moved to Molly's head and in what Charlotte termed 'cowspeak' softly murmured into a reluctant ear, 'Inside lassie, inside you go my dove!' Other cows followed her back into the court and Charlotte bolted them all inside. John looked up at the broken cable.

'And what the hell am I supposed to do about that?' He asked the question not of Charlotte or the mildly curious cows but into the blizzard stinging at his face and neck, with no hope of an answer. After a while he spoke again. 'I'll have to go on the roof, on the lean-to. I think I can reach from there. Go and turn the mains off.' Sensing hesitation, he asked, 'You do know how?' his voice implying that only an idiot would *not* know how.

'We-ell,' Charlotte's mind was blank. She knew about cows and calves, food and drink, and a lot of other things but was vague about electricity. Exasperated, John spoke as if to a child.

'In the cart shed, a door on the left-hand side. Go through and there is panel of switches. Make sure you switch off the mains, the heavy one. Take a torch.'

He turned away, going for ladders. Head down against thickening sleet Charlotte went off to the place where the confusing switches would be. She remembered one for the steading lights, and one for the cottage, but there were so many, for threshing and other things, and she had to find the heaviest. 'Please God!' she implored the whitening world as she approached the arched shelter. The torch gave only a dim light: switches were there all right, begrimed and all very similar, but no, one at the bottom *was* bigger, no doubt at all! She rubbed her hand nervously inside her coat: electricity and damp do not mix, she knew that at least. She pressed the squarish lever which did not move. It must be the one, had to be. She pressed again with all her strength and praise be, it moved slowly and with resistance, but downwards. Pocketing the torch she went back to John.

He was on the roof, well away from the long ladder rattling against the gutter.

'You've turned it off?' he shouted into the wind and Charlotte guessing, though she could not hear, nodded vigorously and shouted back. John reached for the cable–

'Are you *sure?*' Doubt sharpened his voice and then anger. 'You bloody have not!' and curses suitable for the mess-deck of one of Her Majesty's ships flowed thick and fast as he crawled back across the roof, down the swaying ladder and stomped off to do what a useless woman had failed to do. Charlotte, angry enough to abandon the whole operation and John in particular, was too late.

'Hold the ladder!' he instructed, and she obeyed, seething with the injustice of it. He had it coming to him ... later. On the roof John managed to twist together the ends of the cable, looping each end back on itself so there was no possibility of a further break. Slithering and sliding to the ladder, cold and very wet, he came down to earth.

The incident was discussed the following day when Stuart visited them. Charlotte was ready for a sympathetic ear.

'Being spoken to like that! You can't imagine! When I was doing my best! And the language!'

'You still don't get it Charlotte. You near as dammit finished me! Two hundred and forty volts! Ten times more dangerous in the wet!'

'But I *did* turn it off. I pressed the right lever!'

'Not hard enough! You would have heard the clunk! And me on the roof handling live cable! Left on your own God knows how you'd manage...' Words failed him.

Neither expected the mild interruption. 'I dunno John, in these parts a widow-umman with land 'n beasts! She widnae be alane for lang!'

9

Ides

'A few days to go before the deadline, or should I say dreadline?' Charlotte knew John meant the fifteenth of March, which never passed without a comment from her, in fun or with sarcasm, or tentatively when anything unpleasant loomed up. 'Beware the ides of March.'

Far too young to understand anything of them she had skipped through the plays at school, and because the visiting master taking the lessons had no gift for teaching, his classes lapsed into boredom. An exception was the day he read from *Julius Caesar*. Children had been busy with things quite unrelated to the voice of Mr Richards like a bee against a sunlit window droning on and on, trawling the hallowed pages without pause or comment. Ignoring the textbook girls were playing noughts and crosses, or decorating the brown paper protecting their exercise books: some read magazines, others wrote notes to their friends. Mr Richards was either unaware of disinterest or accepted it. Behind a tall old-fashioned desk on a wooden dais he was in every way detached from his charges, requiring nothing of them after he marked them present in a register. Charlotte passed the time sketching, trying to capture the way his beak of a nose twisted at the top and a slight lump that marred the symmetry of his face. She had made a fair job of a downturned mouth and was shading the upper lip when suddenly the master's voice took on colour: words hissed from thin lips dripped menace and stilled the pencils about to make a nought or a cross. Eyes lifted from illicit reading, scribbled notes were left unread.

'Beware the ides of March!' Mr Richards paused, then slowly he warned again, 'Beware the ides of March!'

Illumination did not last. Sadly, Mr Richards could not sustain this new aspect of himself. In the remaining minutes of that lesson and in the following one, throughout the unfolding plot and over the dark deed itself monotony returned and the class busied itself. Charlotte began another sketch and this was not interrupted. Even 'the noblest Roman of them all' brought no glimmer of life. However for her at least the month of March had taken on a new shape.

When John reminded Charlotte about the date both were working at the western boundary of Bithnie land, trying to free a cow entangled in a makeshift fence. Grass was sparse and Bonny had tried to push her way through the barbed wire to reach a neighbouring copse in the hope of an elusive, tasty bite. When the herd returned for the evening feed without Bonny, John feared she might have dropped an early calf; all were heavy in calf but not yet due. Her predicament was less serious but remedying it was painful because barbed wire, possessing a life of its own, was whippy and impossible to control. It paid not to meddle with the stuff without wearing gloves and especially if it happened to be rusty and old, as in this case. The cow stood patiently while they worked. Fortunately her udder was undamaged and other wounds were superficial.

'Good girl,' they kept saying, 'good girl Bonny.' It'd become second nature to talk to cows. Eventually, Bonny decided enough was enough and stepped away, a few remaining barbs smearing blood on her broad red back.

'Good girl,' they said again as she led them home.

'That fence wasn't next on my list but it is now. She's moved it up. Tomorrow I'll start on it.' John closed the gate behind them. As at Burnside, the fences at Bithnie were suspect: was it lack of money or manpower that caused neglect? Or misplaced optimism? Instinctively the other man's grass is always greener to cows and the sun shines bright upon the other side. Maybe this message had saturated the airwaves as cows grazed, or did cows inspire the songwriter? John and Charlotte had found neighbours' animals grazing their parks and had retrieved their own from foreign soil. Agreeing that stout fences make good neighbours they put piky wire and strong posts on the shopping list and considered the money well spent. It has to be said that such a concept was rare in John's thinking since crossing the border and more particularly after taking on a large overdraft: he became like the Aberdonian of folklore and looked at 'baith sides o'a bawbee'.

Barred from the far western park, the herd had insufficient grass, so while John loaded the small cart with his fencing gear Charlotte went to examine the field adjoining the high braes. It was necessary to do this because some walkers showed scant regard for the Country Code. The glint of a jagged tin in a stream near a picnic place; a fence damaged because it was easier to climb over than go to a gate; treks made through growing corn; gates left open. Once she followed a family – mother, father and two little girls, colourful in country clothes, smiling and happy as they walked along. She watched them discard the silver paper from bars of chocolate, regardless of the danger to calves that they thought so very sweet. Charlotte found remnants of balloons launched in support of a charity or to mark some special event: young stock could not survive swallowing these. Checking was vital and had become routine before moving the herd to fresh grass.

Climbing the brae she looked over into adjoining Forestry land and saw, blinking as it left the dark of close-planted conifers, a fox. Becoming aware of Charlotte it stopped and for long moments they stared at each other. She saw gleams of pale sun on a tawny back, a sharp pointed head, slanted eyes scanning her face. She kept very still, rewarded when tiring of her it began to play. A pounce; something tossed up and juggled between swift paws; a frolic on two legs until the thing was lost; a puzzled wait, like a puppy with feet spread, tongue lolling, a plume of a tail waved from side to side. On the back to squirm on the greening turf, with belly exposed, stick legs poking the air. On four feet for a brisk shake. Then, just as suddenly as it came, it trotted back into the dark.

Charlotte stood, trying to crystallise a memory, something she had read: the young fox 'a golden avatar' after a winter, 'slow and dense with cold'. Always there were words which fitted if you could place them. From Louis MacNeice, she thought, but would look it up. She finished the check and walked slowly back to the steading, deciding she would mention the fox only to John. Nearby lived a keeper who shot anything that moved – at any rate that was 'the speak'. They would have to be extra careful of the geese and unfortunately they had taken on another set, a gander and two geese. A friendly postie, looking at the fine Bithnie geese, had told Charlotte a sorry tale of others penned in too small a space. A young couple had fallen for fluffy goslings, having no idea of the true nature of geese. Appalled as the goslings grew large and uprooted plants and splattered all over the place spoiling what used to be a pretty garden, they had put them into a small back yard. Geese need not only water and a warm spot to preen and doze, but are wanderers: the Bithnie gander and his dames ranged far and wide, returning to the Dutch barn for their resting place. Charlotte could not resist offering a home for the disgraced set, could not bear the thought of them in the back yard. Delivering the geese, the man rather shamefacedly said he and his wife did like them but could not cope, and their neighbours hated the noise. The young woman volunteered that the gander knew his name was Solomon or Solly and his wives were Milly and Molly, then with profuse thanks they drove off.

The Bithnie geese were not too happy about the asylum seekers and made sure they knew their place. Disconsolate they trailed at a distance, returned to the barn but dozed apart. At night they were shepherded into the old hut to much chuntering from their betters.

The fifteenth day of March passed: there were minor setbacks but nothing of import. Charlotte noticed that John was amused by something but did not ask, knowing it was bound to surface eventually. There was to be a farmers' meeting at the Forbes Arms so he had little time to shower, change and eat. Leaving the house he turned and said casually, 'By the way, the diary might interest you, have a look at it.'

The entry read: 'I, John Grey, fully aware of this date, the fifteenth day of March, was duly alarmed when Solomon the gander was missing. With some perturbation I began to search, knowing a fox had been sighted. To my great relief I discovered Solomon in the Dutch barn and hereby report that he has LAID AN EGG.'

10

Lees

At the Forbes Arms the farmers had drunk whisky and chased it down with beer, a new one on John with RN drinking habits. The discussion was mainly about the big boys rearing Charolais beef for the supermarkets, anathema for one who loved the Aberdeen Angus breed.

'Guess what!' he said when he got home, 'another chap told me he just missed getting Bithnie!'

'That must be the third one pipped at the post!' mused Charlotte.

The Scottish system of buying and selling

property was different. After discussing things with your banker you made an offer, often somewhere between the figure a seller wanted and what you judged to be the market value. This element of guesswork meant a wild variation in the offers received. An owner would select from those sent to his solicitor before a set time and date and the winner was notified: others found out somehow that they had lost. As in all human exchanges, funny things can happen, and did, when Burnside went on the market. You had to be canny.

'What did you say this time?'

'I said, "Oh, you lucky bastard! You might have had coos die on you, your head bashed in and your nose broken, not to mention a loving wife try to kill you" … or did I say … "Er, really?" Can't remember. One or the other!'

'You could have said your wife only tried to kill you once, and hasn't made a habit of it, yet!'

They were looking at the riverside parks where flooding had left the ground wet and sloppy but the day was mild. If winter had not finished with them and it snowed again tomorrow, this was respite. The Don no longer threatened and a breath of soft air cancelled the memory of tumbling, ice-choked waters. On the same patch of grass they saw two hares, seagulls, oystercatchers and lapwings. In the Doric Charlotte thought they might be bauds or mawkins, seamews, peesies, teuchats. Craigie Step, the old croft at Burnside, had once been 'Teuchatshoose': house of the lapwings, and on its land an old ploughman had stepped wearily from his machine to mark with a stick each place where an oystercatcher had nested. But what was the word for oystercatcher? At Bithnie there was more land, woods unexplored as yet but the same or similar things would happen as the story unfolded.

They walked on, skirting the wood and entering unfamiliar ground bordering the river. Cattle could not be given access to this place; John had renewed fencing to keep them out. Growth suffocated by brambles, threaded by twisting convolvulus, deadened by ivy. Tall trees struggling for light. Some had fallen, their roots with smothering clumps of soil reared at the side of gaping holes. These holes, mysterious and deep, troubled the imagination. What was there in blackness you could not penetrate? A perfect home for fox, or badger, or something rare, more sinister, better left unseen? Charlotte

86

walked on leaving John to clamber down and find nothing at all.

Pools of water close to the river bank and a reedy, swampy part they could not cross, and further into the trees a clearing bright with primroses, and oddly a few of the creamy petals had deepened into shades of pink and delicate mauve. Celandines galore, windflowers, the promise of bluebells and later still the briar rose. An enchanting place, the wild wood, and it looked as though John and Charlotte would leave it, as others had done, to look after itself.

Returning to the house they saw a Land Rover going down the farm road and the driver must have seen them because at the bridge he turned his vehicle and came back. They waited and did not recognise the man who got down and walked towards them.

'A very fine place you have here sir!' he began and surprisingly was not trying to sell anything. 'I do not recall meeting you or your good lady before but I'm a regular visitor to these parts, known to all the farmers, and it's common knowledge that I give a fair price for anything you might want to sell.' He smiled a rueful little half-smile, before going on. 'Now, I was knocking at your door a little while back and I could not help seeing through the window. You'll have to forgive me, but I was very struck by the chairs you have there. May I be so bold as to ask whether you would consider parting? Selling them to me?'

The accent was the same as the young vet who talked in a similar way, but from this man's smart clothes came the whiff of the saloon bar. John asked civilly, 'May I know your name and what firm you represent?'

'Of course sir, of course!' He fumbled and found a card but did not offer it. 'My name is Stout, Michael Stout. As you see, Stout by name and stout by nature!' The laugh was a practised, good-natured one. 'And I am my own master, have my own business. Antiques and fine furniture, which is why I'd like your chairs...' He made as if to put the card away but John reached out and took possession.

He read the card. 'Mr Stout, I must tell you I neither buy nor sell at my door!'

More information was offered quickly. 'You see sir, at my home I have a dresser, a very good piece which might have been made for your chairs, the perfect match I would say. And wouldn't I love to match them up. Six have you? I would be generous...'

'They are not for sale, and if you'll excuse...'

'Four hundred and fifty pounds? Or to clinch the deal I might go to five hundred, though I'd be cutting it fine?' He looked from one to the other and then lowered his voice. 'Cash. All in cash! I understand your situation!'

'As I said, the chairs are not for sale.'

They watched the Land Rover leave.

'Interesting!' John stood at the door and as expected could not see the chairs. 'A pity but we'll have to start locking the door...'

'You filched the card very neatly,' Charlotte offered.

'Yes! I don't filch very often but I am good!' John had not quite given up on Mr Stout. He went to the telephone and dialled the Birmingham number printed on the card.

'Is that Fairways Antiques? Could I speak to Mr Stout please?'

The answering voice was young and uncertain. 'He's nut heeyah.'

'Could I speak to someone else in the shop then? About some chairs?'

'Naaow. Theeres nowbody heeyah. It's jist a 'phown number loike, nut a shop. We tyke missidges fer Mr Stout sumtoimes.' John thanked Marlene and put the telephone back in place.

'As I thought. Not quite right!'

'He must have walked round, peering in every window!' Charlotte did not like the idea.

'It wouldn't hurt to give the police a ring, they could be interested.'

'Just in case,' she agreed.

It did not hurt because it was difficult to speak to the police. Alford, Lumsden, Aboyne. No result. Finally an answerphone for a recorded message.

'A good job it was not too serious. Only a chap who may or may not be a con-man!'

A different thought struck Charlotte. 'It is nice to know really. If you electrocuted anybody. On purpose I mean. You'd stand a fair chance of getting away with it!'

11

Tyauve

The year was taking on a now familiar pattern: calvings, the preparation for hay and silage, the planting. At Bithnie, with extra land and increased stock they needed to use contracted labour more than at Burnside. Bithnie had at one time employed a grieve or foreman who lived in the cottage and several full-time labourers, but those days were gone. Most farmers used contractors, which in the long run was cheaper than buying machinery and employing men, especially when the help was needed for a short period only, say at harvest time. A combine-harvester costing thousands of pounds was not a practical proposition for a man who grew a few acres of barley to feed his own cattle. A natural progression from this situation was a number of small contracting businesses offering man and machine for any of the farm operations. Also there were farmers in a small way who by offering contract work managed to keep their own enterprises afloat and provide work for sons and daughters the farm could not otherwise support.

A neighbouring farmer had previously worked on Bithnie land and over a cup of tea in the kitchen was discussing things with John. The arrangements were sealed with a dram of the stuff usually taken at such times. Mr Dees was a large man, slow spoken, with a wary look about him. He had two sons who helped him on the farm and with contracting as a sideline. The sons were different in character, one dour and uncommunicative, the other outgoing with a ready smile and a joke. Mr Dees was one of three who had 'just missed' Bithnie, but this was not mentioned. The work to be done was the planting of fifty-two acres of barley to be undersown with grass seed. When he was about to leave, Mr Dees had turned to Charlotte and said his wife would be pleased to have a visit but added cautiously, 'If you ring up first.'

Calving had started and so far things had been normal, John or Charlotte present at each birth but not really needed. The new mothers were gated off with their calves in the Dutch barn, an unpopular move so far as the geese were concerned, who thought the place belonged to them. Neither was it good in respect of the small amounts of hay and straw remaining in the barn. Nothing eatable can ever be judged out of reach of a cow, who, while standing on hind legs, can with her strong head push, shove and dislodge anything from a stack. With stolen hay and deep straw to lie on, the new mums had a pleasant time and made an idyllic picture, heavy bodies at rest, jaws rhythmically moving, the sunlight slanting over them and the tiny calves huddled close.

During this first calving at Bithnie friends from the South paid a visit, stayed in the cottage and as envisaged by Charlotte came to the farmhouse for an evening meal cooked by her. Relaxed and happy to chat over old times they were sharply jolted into reality by the noise of an animal, of an animal in great pain. It was a heifer, a purebred Angus calving for the first time. John, annoyed to think he had not expected this to happen, cursed under his breath for being distracted by the visit. Alarm at something quite beyond their experience showed clearly on the faces of the guests. They followed John and Charlotte outside, the food no longer important to anyone. At this late stage the heifer would not be separated from the many curious and interested cows. When they attempted it she stumbled away up the brae bellowing loudly, provoking general hysteria, the others prancing and galloping in her wake. Charlotte urged the visitors to go back into the warm house; there was no point in them hanging about on the damp brae. There was nothing anyone could do but wait, and she and John were used to that.

From the moment when, with a final anguished bellow, the heifer dropped her calf everything went disastrously wrong. She was in shock, bewildered by what had happened to her. Cows overwhelmed by excitement began to interfere, crowded her, anxious to lick a half-alive creature the mother ignored. It took minutes to drive them off and with difficulty get her out of the field. It was a very bad sign that she showed no mothering instinct. Somehow they got her to the steading and into a stall formerly used when fattening a tethered beast. Distraught still, trembling, suspicious of them, she tore avidly at hay they put in a manger and again they waited. The calf lay inert, wet with birth fluids normally licked off by the mother. Charlotte went to make a glucose drink: taken from a bottle with a teat this might stimulate the calf to suck. And that was the rub. There was no way the heifer would allow it. She went crazy when they tried to put the calf on her, backed away, then forward at a rush to butt the poor wee thing out of her life. They shouted and forced her away, scooping up the calf out of her reach. Truly there was a problem.

It was essential for the calf to have colostrum, the milk a cow gives immediately after parturition. This contains more protein and fat than normal milk and is rich in vitamins. The young animal also gets from it

94

antibodies which protect it from bacteria and viruses. There was nothing for it but to immobilise the heifer. Haltered, roped and chained, with a metal restrainer clamped on her back, she could not hurt the calf. A little cunning and a good deal of patience, kicks which missed by a hairbreadth, a hand trapped painfully against a metal gate, and the job was done. Unlicked and unloved, the calf was a beauty, larger than usual for a first calf, which probably accounted for the trauma. They put beet nuts in the trough in front of the trussed animal and while she attacked these goodies, blessedly the calf got that vital suck. It had been exhausting for all of them: heifer, calf and farmers.

Up betimes and the process repeated. Beet nuts as a bribe and the calf suckled, but not without halter, restrainer, chains and ropes, all necessary. No shred of doubt: this was an unwilling and dangerous mother, even a murderous one. They dare not leave the calf anywhere near her. It was going to be a time-consuming affair at the worst possible stage of calving, with more than half the main herd and other heifers yet to give birth. In fact, within hours another heifer produced a small, not very strong calf. However, this animal knew the calf was hers to care for and was anxious to do so, but she would need help. They had a problem mother bursting with milk she hated to give and a second with little except a strong instinct to nourish. One big calf denied normal care; a puny little one with care lavished on it. Both must survive.

They snatched sleep when they could, not necessarily during the night hours. This was normal, a matter of pride to keep a close watch on every animal. Somehow they managed three sessions each day with the imprisoned pair, the same restraints, the same bribes, and an extra task of scything grass. The visitors were delighted to do this grass cutting but hated to witness the restraining process. Farm life, imagined so idyllic, so splendid a retreat from a harsh world, had in one fell swoop lost its appeal. On the third day, John decided to remove the metal restrainer from the heifer's back when he judged the calf had fed sufficiently. Charlotte was ready to pull the little bull away in case of a kick. No kick. A hopeful sign? In a way, but later they had to protect him from a really vicious attack when John did exactly the same thing at the same stage of the feed. It was disheartening and left no alternative to the now routine trussing up.

The visitors departed, more calves were born, and there was a lot of rain, good for grass and not so good for the newborn. Space in the Dutch barn extended, geese retreating noisily from nesting places. Charlotte normally used their wonderful eggs for baking, an irrelevance now. They gave the heifer more room in the steading and dared to open the door of the place where the calf had his bed. The mother did not go in but neither did she seek to ill-use him, an advance of sorts. She became less belligerent and submitted to restraint more easily. A few days later they detected a flicker of interest in her offspring but she was unwilling to feed him. By an ingenious use of gates and fence posts John gave her access to a patch of grass close to the steading, from where she could also see the cows in the Dutch barn. He disliked isolating any animal and took a great deal of trouble to give some sort of contact if this had to be done. Their next attempt at feeding the calf was a failure; the usual bribes could not tempt her, she was full to the brim on lush grass. It was hard not to feel aggrieved as they staggered over at midnight to try again. Happily, next day things went well. A day later she was so quiet that John risked her without the neck chain. The extra freedom and the good grass had helped after all. They gave thought to the next step: softly, softly would be the way.

They treated a young bullock for persistent coughing. A cow produced twins and suckled both, but only regular checks could ensure this continued; sometimes the first-born became dominant and the second twin lost out. There was a scare with Poppy who had previously rejected a calf but this time, after being put into the crush for a clean up, she conformed. Often in a messy state and always needing close supervision, Poppy could be described as 'labour intensive'. Trouble with calves scouring had to be dealt with. At Burnside they had tablets prescribed by the vet. Of course you had to catch your victim, and a 'scoorin' cawfie' could be 'swack as a lop'. When you had him firmly held, with opened jaws and your thumb holding down his tongue, you aimed a tablet at the back of the throat. A newer remedy was in a tube and while chasing the patient remained the hard part, a squirt over the throat, unlike a tablet, could not be manoeuvred back into the mouth, hidden and spat out later. The tubes cut out repeat performances.

They decided to miss out the lunchtime

feed and give the heifer a rest and something of a chance, and this appeared to work. The evening found her standing quietly with the calf sucking. Hardly able to breathe, they watched. Her feet lifted now and again but the calf moved back, waited and then went to the teat again without being harmed. Blessed, blessed moment, when they might be free of the grind of it. They allowed the calf out and watched him settle on the grass. She grazed and afterwards rested but at a distance, showing no interest. He dozed, full of milk, content in an unnatural situation, unaware that he should have been licked, groomed and cossetted as the fine specimen he assuredly was. It seemed better not to read too much into the new situation and in any case they were too busy to change anything.

And then it rained. They saw the little bull trying for the udder while she ranged back and forth over her limited space, and she did not stop, was near to rounding on him to end the pestering. Inside the steading it was the same, she simply did not want to suckle him. Only narrowly did they fend off the kicks.

'Back to square one?' John asked a downcast Charlotte. 'Dylan Thomas,' she replied. 'He wrote something about all there is to give ... "Crumbs, barn..."'

'And halter!' he said, reaching for it.

It took twenty-six days before the bonding was complete. At odd times they spoke of the heifer's arrival on the farm, one of three pure-bred, bought expensively. The young things had kept together as if glued, and remained so close they were given new and obvious names. It seemed ironic that she was chosen for 'Charity'.

12

Blessin's

When a cow was calving it could be a smooth process, as if the cow had read the book and followed all the instructions perfectly. It could be different, with things going very wrong as Charity clearly demonstrated. Weather was important when patrolling the herd to check and check and check again. The soft early green of leaves, a profusion of wild flowers, grazing cows, their calves plump-heaped, or flat with stick legs outstretched, all gave a boost when the sun shone. Late at night familiar things were changed, deep shadowed to disturb, though a moon could turn the river into a silver ribbon and light up the groups of cattle, bonded and mysterious in sleep. Daybreak saw muted colours, glinting beads of moisture on spiders' webs and knotted wire, the lifted nose of a waking animal, a pheasant whirring into flight, but mostly gave the balm of silence.

Rain made a total change and at Bithnie, summer rain did not fall gently. Swathed in oilskins, head down, oblivious of drenched green, defeated blossoms or any spoiled beauty, they squelched along the paths to find animals clustered under bordering trees or pressed against the stone dykes while the heavens downpoured. It could be cold, with a sneaky wind and it was bad for small creatures. The 'scoor' or diarrhoea quickly affects calves who are chilled and wet. Sometimes John brought the herd back under cover to dry out, using both Dutch barn and steading spread with the small amount of straw they had left. Scouring calves were treated then, given tablets or a similar dose from a tube. Whoever had the ingenious idea of putting the 'scoor stuff' into a tube deserved reward, a knighthood at the very least – all 'trauchled fermers' were grateful. It became foolproof, a calf no longer able to regurgitate tablets and keep them hidden in the mouth. After squirts from a tube there were no pink lozenges to find and pick from the straw, no puzzle, no 'whodunnit'. This helped: even a slightly diminished workload was welcome.

There came a time when only a few cows had not calved and John took the opportunity to go to Aberdeen. He had one or two things to do there – first to leave at the Inland Revenue offices tax forms conscientiously filled in but well overdue. He hated to be adrift with any correspondence and particularly so when the chief inspector of taxes, interested in their change to a farming life, had been helpful from the start, guiding them through the different tax system. They had talked about cows and about their first calf which came during a raging blizzard. They had found the cow isolated on high ground, unable to give birth because her calf was 'erse fust'. In a makeshift shelter, while Charlotte held a lamp and book of instructions, John had managed to turn the calf, saving its life and probably the cow's. In return they were told how, also in the depths of winter in an isolated house, Mr Laird's wife had gone into labour. After frantic calls to doctor, hospital and ambulance service, things moved so fast that he had to deliver the baby. When an ambulance, struggling through great drifts of snow, finally arrived, he had opened the door to the men and fainted. They revived him before seeing to his wife and child. All too human then and not in any way like the general idea of a tax man, he had smoothed their path.

John had other errands: from the Farmers' Co-operative on the Esplanade a supply of mineral powder and wellington boots for Charlotte, to replace ones found to leak; from Boots' Agricultural Division nearby, medicines and udder cream. He took a quick look in Bissets where they had antiquarian books as well as others, but resisted temptation. Or was he afraid of Charlotte's stern eye? Wrestling with the tax forms and well aware of expenses to come, she was very conscious of the fragile state of their finances. In the old days he had been good at surprise presents, now he had to calculate before buying her a box of chocolates. A few groceries picked up at Asda and then a call at the Agricultural Training Board offices. He and Angus, the boss there, had planned lunch at the nearest pub. He was more than ready for a drink and a bite to eat.

Old fashioned, a mahogany bar with polished brass rails, food with no frills but large helpings, it was the sort of place they both liked. Approaching the bar, John saw a face he knew reflected in the glass behind it and turned to confirm.

'Chap over there,' he said slowly, 'leather jacket, long hair, has owed me a few bob for more than a year!'

Angus had a look and raised an eyebrow. As of one mind they moved. Leather jacket was sitting with a lady who did not look like his wife. John and Angus stopped, one at each side of his chair. The face raised first to one and then to the other paled visibly.

'I think you owe me some money?' John's voice was very quiet. There was scrabbling in the pocket of the smart coat and a nervous hand brought out a cheque book. Profuse excuses and apologies as the pen slid to complete the cheque. Leather jacket left the lady and the premises. Angus and John walked back to the bar trying not to laugh.

'Funny chap that!' John said.

'Oddball!' Angus agreed.

They enjoyed a very satisfying plough-man's lunch.

Back home John unloaded all his purchases and gave Charlotte the cheque for twenty pounds made out in her name.

'There you are,' he said. 'Spend it on fripperies.'

'But ... who is...?' She tried to decipher the signature. 'Don't ask,' he said. 'Like your old friend used to say, take it as a gift from God.'

13

Bulls

It looked as if the days of 'Rentabull' were over. The different Charleys had come and gone but by now there was a danger that any good heifer kept for breeding could be served by her own parent. So the question was uppermost again – what bull and where to buy?

John was reluctant to use one of the Continental bulls which were gaining in popularity because their progeny fetched high prices at the mart. He disliked the idea of ill-matched pairing which carried a risk to the cow: to him it was against nature to ask a small animal to produce a massive calf from a giant bull. Like to like had been the tradition which had served well in the past and he certainly did not want his couthy Angus cows to have a shorter life through his own need for more income. Other cows in his herd, particularly the original Carnegie stock, were big and hardy but another thing to consider was taste. Pink, bland, lacking the marbling that helped to roast the perfect joint, in his opinion Charolais beef was a disaster. But what was the answer? Was there a happy medium? They discussed the issue with farmers, some quite happy to use the French bulls; with visiting Department people; with the vet who saw the tragic consequences of an ill-advised choice; and of course with Gil and his father from the Burnside days and with the grieve from Carnegie.

Sandy, that staunch and good friend, had something to say which at first made them smile but in reality proved very useful. 'Ask yersel' this question folks – "Has he got an honest face?" It had sounded naive at first and slightly ridiculous until you thought and saw the sense of it. Sandy elaborated: 'It's theer John, if ye look. Jis' like oorselves. Think o' the sneaky bastards ye come across wha dinnae face up tae ye, aye squint te one side or anither or doon at thir feet, onnythin' bit look at ye straight. Then ye meet a body wha looks at ye open faced and somehoo ye git the feelin' I can trust this laddie.' Though it would never enter his head Sandy himself, honest as the day, was the living proof of what he was telling them.

With the exception of one incident with the first Charley who had been provoked into a fight by circumstances outside their control, the Maclean bulls had been easy to handle at Burnside. Charlotte, at first terrified to go near, seeing them stolidly calm, biddable and responsive, was won over. In the end she could be found talking softly while smoothing out flat clustered curls or brushing the shining sides and back of a Charley confined to winter quarters. Miracles can happen, as John never failed to point out.

To the normal perfections hoped for in a bull – breeding, conformation, size and weight – they added an honest face. Travelling to the north around Inverness and south as far as Border country, early or late they looked, prepared to pay a high price for the right animal described in all the literature as 'half the herd'. They saw lively bulls under-used with few cows to serve, and others flagging and plainly outfaced by the work expected of them. Young and old, massive and undersized, Continental and home-bred were seen and noted. They saw cows lean after calving with monster offspring tugging at them and very young heifers with whippet calves that the farmer said grew rapidly. It was confusing. Tired by a day's work before a journey, Charlotte sometimes saw the breeds blurred into one enormous and unlovely amalgam inferior to the known and loved black bull.

They went back to look at the Angus, not at Carnegie as none were for sale there, but a visit to a nearby breeder was hopeful. On the telephone he told them of Canadian bulls he had imported, bigger and better than the natives he said. It was quite late when they drove up to the farm, an impressive house as befitted a man who had sold animals to the Queen Mother and was pictured at her side looking pleased. They walked into a field to see cows with calves at foot also for sale. For Charlotte it was not a happy experience: a cow suckling a fairly new calf caught her attention and she became the focus of another cow hostile to the presence of strangers. Only a bruising push in the back saved her from the charge of this maenad. Bulls in the next park were not suitable for Bithnie: handsome but too young, they had yet to grow to size.

However the promised magnificence of the Canadian imports was ahead.

Evening shadowed the sky. The scent of wettish grass and drenched hedges overlaid the sweetish odour of damp cattle as they went through a final gate to find Canada. And there on the crest of a hill were three grazing bulls...

It was something of a shock that in outline they were unlovely. Long legs and a high rump, a head dwarfed by extra body height. Something of a parody of the sturdy four-square traditional Angus. Odds were against these animals appealing to the Queen Mother. With polite thanks to the owner John and Charlotte left for home.

With uncertain weather, showery at the wrong times, now and again deteriorating into a thorough downpour, this first year at Bithnie needed a Solomon to judge when to cut hay, to turn, row and bale and get it under cover. Time was slipping by: the first cows calved would need to be served in the interest of the tight calving plan advocated by the College. It was frustrating beyond words that a Bithnie bull remained a figment of imagination that would not take shape. Despite a sum of money put aside for the purchase, a vast amount of ground already covered in the search and a growing readiness to adapt, they had achieved nothing. And then someone mentioned Australian bulls.

John Grey sent for details of the Murray Grey breed and liked the look of bulls pictured. He read:

'The thing you notice first about Murray Greys are the colours, from softest silver to fullest grey.' And 'How gentle and peaceful they are. And all cattlemen know that docility is money.' And 'It is the claim and it is probably true, that these are the gentlest cattle on earth.'

Addresses of Scottish breeders who had imported Murray Greys were given and one was within reach. Like the title of a treasured book on John's shelves, it was a case of 'Action this day'.

14

Smasher

They took tea with the man who had chosen to import Murray Grey bulls. While his wife poured and offered biscuits in her comfortable kitchen, Mr David answered the questions John asked and confirmed information given by the Breed Society: he had little fault to find with the bulls he bought.

'Yes, they're quiet enough, important these days. I have fewer men masel'; cannae afford what we had in my father's day.'

Listening, Charlotte suddenly looked down at her teacup and picked another biscuit from the plate Mrs David proffered: it was a shortbread, which she did not eat as a rule, but to her dismay she had found herself applying to Mr David the honest face rule, supposedly for bulls not people, or was it? Another look and she decided Mr David would pass anyway: a brown outdoor face with a grey thatch, a shy man she guessed, not a talker but with a nice manner.

'I'll show you my stock bull, Mr Grey, so you can get an idea of the breed, and also the one I spoke about on the telephone. I aimed to keep him a bit longer. He's nae at his best yet. Over here now...'

They crossed a wide yard towards good stone buildings.

'If you'd stay back Mrs Grey?' At Burnside Charlotte had seen a quiet bull transformed into a whirling dervish and was willing to be prudent. At a distance she waited for the young bull to appear.

It registered in John's mind that the pen was smaller than usual for housing a bull but he was more than surprised when its occupant shot out into the yard like a cork from a bottle. It became apparent that Mr David had no clear idea of what was going to happen next, in fact he too looked astonished. What did happen was to the detriment of a farm cart at one side of the yard. Judging it a fair target the bull set to work and in seconds a side-panel splintered. The tailgate was more resistant but soon left hanging. A final effort upended the whole thing, the contents crash-landing to bounce and spin across the tidy yard. Where next? He snorted off in the direction of ... who else but Charlotte?

Alarm on the faces of Mr David and John,

running... In her head a vague notion that she could deflect him somehow ... shouting worked before when they came across a bull-fight. But it was happening so fast. No time to do anything. Stand quite still. Just stand...

The gladiator stopped.

In a shaky attempt at a normal voice Charlotte spoke:

'Hell's bells laddie! That cart! And me? What've I done?' Her breath returning she tried again. 'Sorry are you? You forgot! Didn't read the book!' She wondered if an English accent registered after Aussies and the Scots.

Apologies from Mr David, mopping at his face, genuinely worried and grateful when she did not make a fuss. All watched as the bull munched goodies hastily provided. He had the right conformation, not quite the size they wanted but he would grow. Totally quiet now, between mouthfuls the great head lifted to inspect the strangers within his gate. Below a high mound of a forehead, wide-set brandy-ball eyes queried. The look was noble and straightforward.

Tentatively the price of the young bull was mentioned.

'He's a fine lad Mr David,' John said without surprise at an amount they could just about afford. In spite of the quiet years at

Burnside, he suspected the aura of London riches lingered and always would. About the farm he wore clothes only marginally better than a tinker's; they did not dine out or socialise much but rumour dies hard: he was until the end of time the chap with a bonnie penny who left the rat race to play at farming. Later he wanted to ask what Charlotte thought of the kerfuffle; had the cart-slaying put her off? He would remind her that one cart at Bithnie was made of steel. After watching Mr David and his grieve take the Murray Grey back to his pen, they went off to see the stock bull.

At home they had a telephone call from Alastair in Aberdeen with news of some Aberdeen Angus bulls. They were not ideal for Bithnie, being aged, but at a reasonable price one of them might fill the gap until the right animal came along. Alastair gave directions: the bulls were in a triangular field just off the Alford-Huntly road before you got to Bridgend. They could be clearly seen from the road – seven pure Angus coming to the end of a working life but proven breeders of good stock. The owner said a prospective purchaser could go into the field to see them at any time, they were quiet auld lads, 'nae bother ava'. Did John think it worthwhile having a look?

John thought so and at the earliest moment pointed the Land Rover in the direction of Huntly. A bull was now urgently needed at Bithnie and it seemed odd that choice rested between extremes – new and over-feisty, or aged and well-tried. An easy place to park the Land Rover and then a short walk down a side road, a gate to lean upon and look. Quite soon John went through the gate to stroll around, appearing to take no notice of the grazing animals. They did not seem fazed by his presence: he might have been their owner doing a routine check. After a little while he went alongside the nearest beast and gently laid a hand on his back, then paused before sliding aft to give a good scratch at the tail head. This manoeuvre worked as a rule and did not fail now. Up came a massive head with a greying cluster of curly hair, a blissful mouth dripped saliva, eyes became slits: it was ecstasy. Other bulls were moving in his direction. John stood for a while and then stepped closer. He repeated the friendly stroking, patting and back-scratching, talking softly in what Charlotte called his steading voice. In turn each animal's age was assessed along with its response to John's blandishments; the face judged; the working gear beneath each heavy bulk closely examined. Except in one case.

The last of the bulls had not moved with the others and was not grazing. John had a strong impression of being watched. He walked away from the group and round the perimeter of the field, making an approach slowly and from another angle. The last bull had not moved and still did not take any grass. Closer, John stopped and met the stare of the waiting animal. It was something of a shock. Never before had he seen a look of such brooding malevolence: heavy-lashed eyes projected evil, sent an ice sliver into the heart, a tremor down the spine. Whatever shaped this animal had been brutal, leaving him bereft of goodwill. He was not likely to accept friendliness. His tail would remain unscratched by John or anyone. It was a pity. Sullen and uncompromising against a heavy sky, an aged defiant creature whose future looked bleak indeed. The other old boys? Well, perhaps they would have better luck.

The image of the bad old bull lingered for John and gave Charlotte a chance to tease. 'Was it a very squinty look then? Sort of anti-English? SNP maybe?'

For once he had no answer. 'There was just something...' he admitted, but could

116

not elaborate.

They went again to see Mr David's bull, this time in a paddock behind the house. With jaws rolling after grazing his fill of good grass, he looked quiet and content, his noble head held steady, the powerful neck muscles relaxed. On a rare day of sunshine for the first time they saw the beauty of his colouring, a pale gold with an almost pinkish cast enhanced by the effect of water-marking, faint outlines glowing as shot silk does against the light. With some pride Mr David told them the pedigree name which was shortened for everyday use to 'Goldwater'.

They left for home where Charlotte, filling in the diary, wrote: 'We have bought a pink bull'.

15

Tummelt

As well as the good strong cross-bred cows in the herd at Bithnie they had a mini-herd of pure Aberdeen Angus cows started at Burnside when John bought Eva-Jan with calf at foot. He had been well and truly twitted about what was considered to be the purchase of a luxury item but now, seeing the compact little band of good animals, people were not so ready to criticise. The pure Angus had won approval from the high-class trade, the gourmet eaters in the expensive restaurant bracket. All the cows on the farm were well cared for and got close attention when 'fairing' to calve but with the Angus there was also an element of self-justification. They could not afford mistakes with any cow and where an expensive bought-in animal was concerned it was more stressful. When Emma-Jan was ready they decided on artificial insemination from a top-class bull. Inevitably a nail for the AI man's breeks was suggested by the wags. 'I wish folks 'ud grow up!' John said irritably, picking up the telephone to dial the number of the Aberdeen office. Soon afterwards a man from the Milk Marketing Board brought semen given by the splendidly named El Cordobez of Dunkeld and left with a cheque which included VAT. The job took only minutes; they had perfected a handling system at Burnside and the inseminator was adept. Months went by, the move to Bithnie had taken place and now the moment was near. Emma-Jan would complete the year's calving at the new farm. With luck El Cordobez would give a heifer calf to add to the pure stock.

John had promised to help Gilbert and his father at their brucellosis test and a summons came when he did not want to be away for any length of time.

'Promise you'll ring me if she looks likely?' he asked, and Charlotte agreed though she could not imagine him dashing away from the stramash of such a day. When their own test came they would call upon Gilbert to help; it was a reciprocal arrangement which had worked well at Burnside, and all hoped it would continue, though the farms were further apart.

Charlotte watched the Land Rover jolt off down the farm road to cross the Bailey bridge. Tric-trac, tric-trac, those clattering planks were useful as a sign of anyone approaching the farm; 'the gypsy's warning' John sometimes called it when he was tired and felt unsociable. She decided to go and have another look at Emma-Jan, though John had checked all the cows before he went off. There was a busy day ahead because of all unexpected things, friends on a brief touring holiday were coming to lunch the following day. It was natural to want everything to be

119

perfect: lunch, the house, the farm, and of course it wouldn't be. The last time Charlotte cooked for guests, excessive drama was provided by Charity and went on interminably. Fingers crossed it won't be like that tomorrow, she prayed. Really, it was unlikely. Fussed over from the moment of her arrival on the farm, petted, groomed like a show animal, Emma-Jan had been a sort of trophy, part of John's luxury spend. Tame and biddable she was different in every way from Charity but one never knew. It was necessary to check and keep checking. A pity they had not been able to bring the heifer close to the house, but the little paddock was now occupied by Goldwater. She smiled at the thought of the pink bull and quickened her steps along the path which led to the Angus cows.

It was a favourite walk because it gave a clear view of the low pastures. Someone long ago had planted the trees bordering the river, had pictured their matured beauty and the merciful shade given to cattle in summer's heat. Reaching out in such an act of faith was rare and in the confusions of today seemed impossible. Stone dykes were another legacy from the days when a farm employed its own builder at small cost. Now it was a specialism: a wall could be built to last for decades but at a price beyond most farmers. So, regretfully, dykes were patched up and eventually replaced by piky wire fences offering no shelter at all from sun or harsher winter weather.

Today the sunshine was lovely. Harebells of transparent blue nodded from sparse grass on top of a retaining wall on the path's upper side. Sedums, more aptly called 'wall-peppers' lifted tiny star-like flowers above growths of moss subtly different in shape and colour. Patches of blaeberry brought a fleeting thought of their blue-black fruit later, in a pie ... and the pastry she must make for tomorrow if all was well. The main herd was in the wood, where they found the sweet vernal grass local people called 'natural' grass. Lucy lifted mild eyes as Charlotte passed. Lucy, 'the friendly cow, all red and white I love with all my heart...' 'How could anyone ignore you, Lucy?' It was unthinkable even today. She lifted a hand to be brushed by Lucy's broad damp nose and a sturdy calf came closer, friendly and trusting like the mother. Standing there she was able to see most of the cows and all seemed well. There was also nothing to see when at last she reached the Angus cows on a brae further along. A glance round but all was in order: Emma-Jan showing no signs at all. Really the trek had been unnecessary.

She hurried back and made an onslaught, tidying, dusting, a spot of polish where it was needed and a thorough attack on bathroom and lavatories. Housework inevitably took second place on the farm but she had made a difference; the place looked nice, particularly the sitting room where they so rarely sat. Tomorrow she would cut roses from the rampant climber round the door. She wanted Lisa to think they led a civilised life, though it was hardly the truth. She was hot and grimy and needed a shower before starting to cook. She had heard a television cook say that organisation was the key: you should prepare as far ahead as possible for any planned meal, and she agreed with that. He also said that the supreme compliment to pay a guest was taking trouble. You gave your most precious commodity, your time. True also, but did he ever have to break off to go and look at a cow?

Clean and refreshed she arranged on the kitchen table the things needed for pastry, and paused for a moment. The room was so tidy as to be unrecognisable. John was sure to remark on that when he got home. He would also be anxious about the cow so she would go back to have another look. It was a nuisance. Why oh why did John have to be away on this particular day? On the high path again, but no time for what the bonny day offered – tiny clustering flowers, a glimpse of the quiet river, of cattle resting now under the green shade – only resentment welling up. Once in a blue moon did they have guests and she wanted time to prepare. John could never see it, the need to have everything right, the meal, the house. She could hear him: 'Get your priorities right, cleaning the house from top to bottom is ridiculous, who cares about a spot of dust?' And the cooking? What about that? 'The lunch is tomorrow, for Heaven's sake! And they are coming to see you and me, not looking for Chef of the Year!' Useless talking to him! She hurried on, brushing thistles as she passed, causing tiny seeds to drift into the balmy air, so delicately, so beautifully, spreading bane, she thought, just like me, and the day is so lovely.

At last the Angus cows and Emma-Jan and it was pretty obvious that she was getting ready. A little way from the other animals, something uneasy about her, an aimless sort of wandering back towards the others and then away from them, her tail lashed rapidly from side to side as Charlotte watched. The

123

birth was going to happen whether convenient or not. So that was that. Not without a sigh she settled against the dyke to wait before taking a closer look. The vulva would be swollen and a clear, straw-coloured stringy mucus secreted, a sign of the preliminary stage of calving. It was time to get the priorities right as John said, 'first things first'. She remembered from the green book that 'the majority of domesticated animals require little or no assistance in the actual feat of parturition' and hoped it would be the case with Emma-Jan. The book also advised that someone should be at hand in case of emergency. Well, here she was, Charlotte Grey, fed up to the back teeth, recognition as 'Chef of the Year' beyond her grasp as always.

After some time Emma-Jan went down then got up almost immediately; several times she did this, kicking at her belly and looking wonderingly at her flank. She resumed the aimless wandering. The pains were stronger: she was anxious, strained, breathing fast, then briefly calm until the next pain struck. If all was well the water-bag would appear. Charlotte thought she glimpsed it, pink, bladder-like between the lips of the vulva. It meant the head and forelimbs were being forced into the pelvis and external genital passage until the hooves reached the vulva. When the water-bag burst there would be respite, a time to gather strength before worse pain and the agony of birth.

It happened. The water-bag protruding further and further and rupturing, a rush of fluid and the forefeet clearly visible, the nose behind them, thank God, as normal. The merciful pause... An Angus cow lifted her head from grazing then continued; a plane droned overhead. Charlotte drew close. Intense concentration, sun, wide sky and the balm of summer as nothing to Emma-Jan, glassy-eyed, still, in another world... Shuddering pains more violent, a supreme effort, and then on the grass, a calf twitching, slithering down the brae, Emma-Jan in panic after it. Quickly, Charlotte bent to clear mucus from the spluttering jaws and wisely stepped back. There had to be no interference even from a friend. But all was well: a wrinkled nose sampled air, a black head wavered, too heavy on a thin stalk of a neck. Frantic licking to obliterate birth fluids and a tiny voice protesting. Thin stick legs with hooves of polished jet struggling to stand, collapsing, persisting until four-square. Nudged to the udder, a tentative mouth, finding, losing the teat. Then again and a flow of milk. Pleasure from a thin slip of a tail lashed against a shiny rump. Loud sucking, a creamy froth at the tiny mouth. What joy! Charlotte in a flood of relief whispering, 'Good girl! Clever girl!' She could not wait to tell John. And there he was, hurrying along the path. Knowing he would look up, Charlotte waved both arms. Climbing, he slowed only when he saw the little black heap beside Emma-Jan.

'All over, John. Nae bother!'

'What is it?'

'Heifer most likely, but I couldn't get too close, she wouldn't have it!'

Confident, he stepped towards the calf and bent to check, but a black arrow sent him rolling, rolling, 'erse over tip' down the brae.

Charlotte did not resist. 'Told you!' she called and couldn't stop laughing. It was something of a comeuppance from a cherished luxury animal.

'Ye ken,' Wullie remarked later, 'it's nae allwyes yir enemy as lands ye in the sharrn!'

126

16

Visitation

'You make too much fuss,' the boss told her as he went off to bed, affronted still by Emma-Jan's rapid despatch of him.

'You don't mind once the serious eating begins,' his wife observed, suspecting there were fewer almond-filled pastries cooling on a wire tray. She hoped these and all his other gleanings would lie in harmony throughout the night or what was left of it. Venison kept for an occasion was to have a pepper sauce which took ages to make; she was almost asleep as she stirred.

By some miracle all was ready and for once haphazard working clothes were discarded for something a little more normal if by no means smart. They watched a long, sleek vehicle negotiate at very slow pace a farm road used to rougher traffic. And then, Lisa and Michael, elegant in the 'right' sort of country clothes seldom seen on working farms. Belonging to another life, dear and familiar, it was lovely to see them. John persuaded Michael into the paddock to look at Goldwater but Lisa resisted.

'Not me, darling, I can see beautifully from here!'

To Michael's patent relief Goldwater showed no animosity, allowed himself to be scratched by John, gave no more than a cursory look from golden eyes at the stranger invading his querencia. Truly the cart-wrecking bull was becoming something of a gent.

Lisa praised everything: farm, garden, house, lunch and also the colour of Goldwater's skin, exactly that of a chocolate praline, she thought. If her appreciation was extravagant that was just Lisa, 'over the top as always' John said later, but you had to like Lisa. Beneath all the froth there was warmth which surfaced. People responded, even while eyebrows shot up at some remark or other. If you divided people into drains and radiators, Lisa qualified brilliantly as the latter. They had spent a few days at a well-known hotel so that Michael could play golf and Lisa had been much taken by someone there.

'He was a laird of somewhere or other, wore the kilt but without swagger as if it

128

were the most natural garment in the world – but then he had lean legs and very little paunch, which must be a help, do you think?'

Here Michael interrupted as he often needed to: 'Do not fear the worst Charlotte, he was about a hundred and ten years old!'

'Don't spoil it Michael!'

The old laird had been full of stories, described coming home from school in his father's first motor car, a marvellous vehicle capable of reaching forty miles per hour, which they never attempted. Few cars were on the roads then but the journey was full of hazard, with hairpin bends where the driver, really their groom, wavered at unfenced edges sloping away into nothingness. They had been used to walking up steep hills to consider the horses: with the new car nerves prompted walking downhill as well. Lisa had been a good listener, charmed by a soft accent and precise diction. The tales would figure in talk of the Scottish holiday, enhanced.

'There was this Scotsman, from an old family...' Twenty or even thirty years would be shed in the telling until the old laird was Braveheart outbraving the Irish star of a Hollywood version of Scottish history. That was Lisa's way and if found out she giggled and admitted, 'Well, you know me, darling!'

Charlotte told the saga of Emma-Jan and John's comeuppance, although she had said, 'We had better steer clear of cowtalk, do you think?' and John had agreed. It was something of a pitfall when preoccupation with animals made the glaze of boredom in non-farming eyes very difficult to see. They drank coffee in a little sitting room rarely used: it had become their 'posh' room, the furniture and pale colours did not fit the life they led. Seen from the window an old-fashioned climbing rose spilled over a beech hedge, a bowl of its scented flowers glowed on the wide sill. Solemnly the grey gander, his ladies and their goslings walked into view and in a moment the adopted trio followed with one tiny yellow ball of fluff stumbling in their wake.

'They shouldn't be in the garden!' John explained, but allowed the procession to pass. They would end up at the back door demanding slices of bread, the gander rapping smartly with his orange beak until answered. It was the custom.

Drying the dishes the boss pronounced the meal 'very eatable'. Sincere praise, though he never refused food of any kind at any time of day or night. A question of refuelling, he would explain, 'You have to keep the engine topped up!'

In former days after a boozy lunch in Lisa's company Charlotte would spend the rest of the afternoon sleeping it off. Now muzzy after wine she opted for fresh air and helping John by checking the animals. He had changed into working gear and would want to make up for lost time.

'Three whole hours off in the middle of the day! How dissolute!' Lisa had teased, hugging him in farewell.

A cool breeze agitated trees by the river, pushing at leaves to lift their silvery undersides. The sky promised rain. The herd was gathered in the narrow part of the wood and she became absorbed in the routine checks, looking particularly at each udder where mastitis, a painful and nightmarish thing to treat, might develop in any teat left unsucked. But Lucy, Blossom, Beauty, Flora, Suzy and the rest were in fine fettle, their calves growthy and brimming with health, Gertie, unusually benign, allowing a brief scratch at the tail. Angus cows on the high brae, Ethra, Isla, Faith, Hope and Charity, Juana, July and Fiann; Emma-Jan, polished new calf asleep in the curve of her body;

131

Eva-Jan guarding them and her own black treasure. All was well.

Charlotte decided to go back by the river, through the wild wood they left to take care of itself. In the springtime there had been windflowers like pale drifts of snow, and she wanted to see what was there now. First the river, lower than normal, pools at the edge specked by darting insects; stones made visible, catching the light. She climbed a wall that once kept animals out. Rotting wire sagged above its tumbled stones. Tall trees close grown, fallen trunks with roots at the edge of holes that seemed bottomless but with new growth everywhere. Digitalis, white, cream, and pink, lingering wild roses, a scented tangle of honeysuckle. Dampness and green mosses starred by tiny flowers. Silence except for small sounds and then emerging from tangled grass a large bird with a pheasant's gliding walk, head flicked from side to side, eyes quick to see. It was pure white. Escaped? A white pheasant was said to be prized by shooting men and left unharmed. As a child Charlotte imagined the mysterious third of the Holy Trinity would be a bird like this one.

The way home was through a park with easy access to the Don, a path bordered by

132

trees with jutting roots and low branches made shiny where cows had rubbed. Here the impacted soil gave off an acrid sweetness from cows refreshed in many a long year.

John was slumped in a favourite chair, work ended for the day, his hope of food almost tangible as he waited. He asked about the cows. Charlotte reported and told him about the low river water and the wood's summer face. He had picked up a newspaper Michael had brought and was only half-listening.

'But Emma-Jan and the calf, you were satisfied?' he asked absently, and then abruptly at her next remark, 'What? What's that you said?'

Smiling, she looked him in the eye.

'Only that I saw the Holy Ghost!' she said.

17

B & B & B

They were waiting for Boris, their old ram from Burnside, and spent the time leaning on the paddock gate looking at Goldwater. A rather large lump in a cluster of cows he was a satisfying sight. All were taking what Charlotte described somewhat imprecisely as their 'elevenses', rest taken after hours of grazing. It was pleasant to see them cudding away, the rhythmic roll of jaws a definite sign of well-being – its absence meant trouble ahead.

A strange and complex process goes on, when food taken earlier is returned to the mouth to get a more thorough chewing before being swallowed again. The invaluable green book gave information that rumination or cudding may have evolved from animals having to eat with great speed in fertile areas where they were likely to be attacked by predators – i.e. they chewed sufficiently to enable them to swallow the food and then retreated to safer ground to regurgitate and chew again. The book went on to say, 'Whether this is or is not true, it would appear that some such provision as rumination is necessary when the coarse nature of the food and its indigestibility are remembered'.

All the early calvers were now with Goldwater, and because oestrus in the cow lasts for only a matter of hours a careful watch was vital to check that he was doing his work. It seemed he was, and as they noted the name of the cow and the date of each encounter it became obvious that the young bull would cope with the whole herd in due course.

More of a relief after the cart-bashing incident, Goldie was proving calm and biddable; they had no problem whatsoever in moving him and his 'girls' when necessary. He was docile and like the others susceptible to blandishment, a 'puckle' of beet nuts worked wonders with them all. John and Charlotte discovered this secret early in life at Burnside.

On moving to Bithnie they decided with some regret to give up on sheep and put all energies into the suckler herd. Any sheep enterprise would have to be more ambitious at Bithnie and there was no time to spare for that; increase in stock would be of cows only. The ram and the old ewes were hefted to the Burnside hill land and Dugald, the new owner, was a sheep man of vast experience. It was a logical and sensible decision to leave them there. However, in the normal exile of a ram from any flock, Boris was coming to Bithnie for his 'holidays'.

It was something of a puzzle as to where he should spend this time. Animals miss the company of their fellows and one solution would have been to put him with Emma-Jan and the Angus cows. But, and it was a very big 'but', Boris was not fond of cows of any breed. It was no exaggeration to say that he was afraid of cows. So, he was for a high park adjoining Forestry land where he could see the black Angus cows without mingling with them. This decision was worthy of Solomon, John thought.

Dugald's Land Rover coped easily with the steep braes to deposit Boris in his holiday area. A Suffolk ram, he seemed to have aged rapidly, becoming an old Suffolk ram whose woolly coat was patchy. It was hinted to them that his appetite rather exceeded his physical capacity. Just for old times' sake Charlotte provided him with a half-bucketful of beet nuts and John tut-tutted, ever mindful of the bawbees.

It had to be assumed that Boris would settle when left to his own devices. Charlotte was a little uneasy about this but in her heart knew John was right when he said, 'He has plenty of room and plenty of food. There isn't much more we can do, it's not our place to provide him with a shrink!'

Work occupied them for the rest of the day and it was not until the following morning that Charlotte had time to check on Boris. Walking along she thought of Burnside when, after a prolonged snowfall, they had found Boris and the old ewes quite safe in a little walled copse, not buried under the drifts as feared. At any minute she expected to see the ram, but oddly drew a blank. He was nowhere in sight. Where the heck was he? One thing was certain, he was not in the designated place and there was nothing for it but to go back and alert John. It was a nuisance, she had enough to do without playing hide and seek. Resisting the impulse to look again over the same ground she crossed a narrow stream bordered by junipers, their branches widespread; surely a ram would not shelter under such an umbrella? No, not Boris. Down then, following the boundary wall here and there damaged by deer or merely by the passage of time. A glance into the plantation: an outer band of deciduous trees and then conifers grown quite close; very little light, a good place for wild things like the young fox she had seen, and for Boris, because the slumbering heap at a distance was undoubtedly the timid ram, a sound which had puzzled Charlotte was his gentle snoring.

In sleep, was Boris a young ram, giant, brave, ranging the hills of home with many ewes, undeterred by horned monsters masquerading as cows? She would leave him cushioned by pine needles, the trespass harmless, easy to explain should a Forestry Commission green Land Rover appear before they got him back. They would have to figure out the best way to do that: she could visualise Boris plunging further into the mysterious depths in response to any move they might make. Perhaps they had better not leave him too long...

'He looked so peaceful John, like a shaggy dog, I wish you had seen him.'

'He would have had a rude awakening if I had!' Then relenting, 'But it will be easier with two...'

It was not all that easy, in fact Charlotte went back to get goodies to lure him from the shadows. And after that, when they had negotiated the only available gateway there was a posse of interested black cows, never indifferent to the rattle of a bucket or a drifting aroma from the prized nuts.

Boris in younger days would have cleared the gate to trespass again but now, alarm in his basilisk stare and almost visibly shrunken, he waited, in dire need of protection. With faltering feet, with piteous glances from right to left and back again, pressing hard against their legs at any move from his enemies, Boris walked between them to the steading and sanctuary in the empty bull pen.

They took a last look at him after the evening check on all the animals and gave thought to a next move.

'He can't go back up there.'

'He's afraid of cows and geese.'

'He would be terrified of Goldwater.'

'He can't go in the garden to eat the lettuces.'

'If we put him in the wild wood he would drop into a hole.'

'We might let him stay in the bull pen for now, but with the gate open, so he can pop in and out, grazing the verges and behind the steading.' Lacking other ideas they did just that.

John heard on the radio a well-meaning Ministry spokesman suggesting that to boost income farmers should look at diversification, perhaps into some enterprise like bed and breakfast for tourists. Financial help might be available. 'Bed and breakfast! Bed and bloody breakfast!' he said.

'Don't get your knickers in a twist, John. I wouldn't dream of it. Too busy!'

'That is the whole point. Imagine them thinking that up, sitting in a fancy office pushing paper about. What would be the reaction to anyone suggesting their wives cooked for tourists or that a part-time job as a waiter would suit them?'

'You sound like a Bolshevik!'

'I am one! Never used to be but it makes my blood boil, all the people who have never in their lives done a job that knackers them, taking every ounce of physical energy, and mental too, because of the economic situation. Not to mention the weather and foreign imports. And they suggest bed and breakfast!'

'I shouldn't imagine it applies to the big boys, only the family farmer.'

'Again you've hit the bull's-eye. The man with thousands of acres does no physical work, employs people. The family farm nowadays is down to the man himself and his wife maybe, but he cannot afford all the labour he needs.'

'You can say that again.' Charlotte spoke with feeling, then to cheer him said, 'Shall I pour us a dram? Not too bourgeois?'

John's day had been rough and a drop of the water of life did help. They lingered, musing on Boris afraid of anything on four legs ... Blackie, the predatory cat ... a gander who laid an egg...

Financial help for B&B. Sheltering a tourist would be a piece of cake compared with getting the heave-ho from Emma-Jan or Charity, admittedly reformed, or Gertie who was not and had the 'cornada' ever in her mind.

Financial help for dealing with that lot? It was unlikely.

18

Wirk

'Good hay, sweet hay, hath no fellow' – though spoken by an ass, it rings true. To 'make hay while the sun shines' is sensible, but older and wiser by far is the saying 'Make your hay as best you may'. Grass cut green but on the point of maturing. A benevolent sun and light winds as the machine tosses and turns it and then with a slight adjustment makes long high-piled swathes to await the baler. Bales left on the greening aftermath before carting dry and sweet-smelling to the barns. All under a cloudless sky of perfect blue ... is the stuff of dreams.

At times John had been desperate and forced to buy in hay. With increased acreage at Bithnie, he determined to produce more than enough so that the surplus could be sold at the high market prices he had paid. Like the weather that year, hay taken varied in quality; some excellent, some good, and a small amount not good at all, but without doubt there was plenty. Large round bales were stacked high in the Dutch barn, but to make use of storage space in the old steading many small bales were taken. The process of stacking these in the fields, then carting and stacking again under cover was back-breaking. An elevator bought and installed earlier proved a blessing, lifting 2,000 bales to the back regions, but more handling was needed there to pile and stack in the separated booths, where tethered cattle were once housed. Hours and hours of work for John, Charlotte and now and again paid casual labour, but John bore the brunt of it. Early and late, from morning as soon as the dews were gone to past eleven at night in the extended light of the northern climate, they took hay 'as best you may'.

A peeping Tom might have seen John strip to plunge into the Don during the hottest spells. There was an all too familiar sinking in the heart if showers fell on a cut field and worse despair when a steady downpour ruined hay ready to bale. Unbearable was the prospect of starting all over again, the blackened hay spread to dry for a long time, vulnerable under heavy skies. A second, third or more attempts with the turner and finally bales to be used early because they would not keep, all quality lost when the heavens opened. This explains why the farmer's ear is always glued to the weather forecast and why 'Bring me Sunshine' is his favourite song.

Anxious examination when a whiff of heat came from anything prematurely stacked. The last bales and muscles that cried 'no more, no more', casual worker Dave handling heavy rain-soaked bales in the field remarking as he sweated, 'These eens are buggers, John!'

Charlotte agreed when the same bales came off the elevator. 'Oh! These are the buggers! Very, very heavy!'

But Wullie, who was giving a hand, picked up one in each hand and carried them off. His grin said all there was to be said.

Pride in that which was good and sweet-smelling, especially the bales in the Dutch barn, neatly manoeuvred by John, now grown expert with the loader. This was ideal storage, under a roof but open to air and wind. This hay'd be used in the worst times. Everyone had a tan not sought or paid for on a foreign beach but acquired in the daily slog. Satisfaction welled up at the crammed steading, the great quantity which meant freedom from anxiety in the winter months, and much relief that in spite of setbacks they had managed once again to make hay.

A move for cows onto the aftermaths of the first fields taken and a day for Charlotte when looking at them was the only task; a blissful day of rest. John not so lucky, away to Aberdeen to collect materials ordered for the next item on the list, heavy-duty electric cable to go underground and replace the dodgy overhead system inherited.

It was a change anyway, driving on a quiet road, the steady thump of a diesel engine from the Land Rover. A sigh, thinking of the Alfa effortless in heavy traffic, practically noiseless in those happy days of 'The Red Streak'. Through Alford and along past an interesting old fortified house near beautifully-named Tillyfourie, and at Sauchen the farmhouse of 'Leggerdale', a blip on the horn to greet good friends there. Dunecht, Kingswells, a little more traffic and clusters of modern housing, and on to the granite city. Crematorium, school, tall houses used as offices for insurance, law, finance, oil. Built by prosperous men for large families, with ample room for the nannies, cooks, parlourmaids and manservants who looked after them. Lives glimpsed sometimes in magazines as of a different world; only the gardens show little change if you ignore discreet notices with the name of a bank or company established in the former home.

At last through busy streets to the industrial area and the cable company yard. Armoured cable, seven-eighths of an inch in diameter cost £500 which was a great deal of money to John but had to be spent. A friendly foreman and a hundred-yard roll hoisted by three men into the back of the Land Rover. The journey home slower because of the considerable weight, John wondering as he drove over the bridge how he, with only Charlotte to help, would manage to unload the massive coil. Charlotte, as he expected, was dismayed by the seemingly immoveable mass wedged tight in the vehicle but after one or two failed attempts they manoeuvred it to the ground and rolled it under cover. A man from Keig who owned and operated a digger, a self-employed contractor they'd used on drainage work at Burnside, was due early the following day to dig a trench. A major item on John's list'd be started and with luck completed before the barley was ready for harvesting.

Steady progress by the digger, and the trench took shape at a depth of three feet for the whole length of the steading and further on towards the farmhouse. The heavy cable was laid along the completed trench with every yard or so a flat stone and a yellow plastic label bearing the words DANGER: ELECTRIC CABLE, an essential warning in case of any future excavations. Backfilling, the earth piled over the laid cable and neatly levelled and the contractor could take his yellow machine back along the narrow road to Keig with a fair day's work behind him.

The connection of the cable to the electricity supply was the next thing for John to tackle, tricky but less cumbersome than what had gone before. Power turned off at the box in the cartshed, making the satisfactory clunk that Charlotte had not achieved on a previous occasion, though neither of them mentioned this. The old cable was disconnected and replaced by the new, its vital copper core heavily insulated within a layer of steel armour and finally by black polythene. To the gable end of the house next and a bracket attachment on a chimney, for the same process of replacing old with new cable, the connection heavily wrapped against the weather. The crucial test then, POWER ON

146

and every house switch ON! Blessedly it worked, the lights pale in rooms full of sunlight but the fridge and freezer boomed away to make up lost time.

Finally the overhead cable was unhooked and brought down, piled into the steel cart and transported to spare ground behind the steading. It was something of a shock to see tattered covering which did not approach the strict standards of insulation now in force. A satisfying fire made short work of the rotting fabric to leave what John knew as 'clean' copper, which he would sell in Aberdeen later to make a little dent in the expense so far incurred. It was never pleasant to think of money going out, even for planned improvements. John never could believe in the old saw, 'Siller's like a muckmidden, it daes nae gweed till its spread'.

No peace for the wicked! John on the road again while Charlotte looked after the cows. A time for rest and recuperation would have been welcome but a cattle-handling system had to be ready for the autumn when their regular brucellosis and tuberculosis test was due. It was unclear how cattle had been managed previously at the farm. No trace of a cattle crush remained, or any system of gates or rails which might have given a clue as to how things were done. Therefore John worked out a plan of operation but again it meant laying out money and getting everything completed before it was time to harvest the barley, fifty-two acres of it.

On order from a firm in Glasgow and due for delivery were lengths of two-inch heavy-duty steel tubing – galvanised scaffolding in fact. A crush gate and extra square metal uprights were on order from the 'lad at Monymusk', the highly regarded blacksmith there. John's errand to Aberdeen was for clips to fasten the lengths of steel tubing and for the hiring of a Kango hammer and transformer, heavy equipment again to be carried in the back of that valued work-horse, the Land Rover.

Holes two feet deep, holes where eight-feet uprights would be concreted in to give a height of six feet for the completed barrier. Growing piles of rubble as the hammer bored through earth to meet solid rock. Ear-shattering noise throughout the days and blessed relief if it stopped even for minutes of rest or for brief mealtimes. Prompt delivery from Glasgow but the articulated lorry could not manage the bridge and had to unload in the layby at the Bithnie entrance. John backed tractor and cart down the road and over the bridge to park as near as possible to the piled lengths for an urgent job of loading, the roadside not the place to leave expensive goods lying about.

'Hard work never hurts anybody'? John and Charlotte often wondered about that little gem of wisdom. Painfully slow across the wooden planks of the bridge, tr-ic–tr-ac, tr-ic–tr-ac, and suspense as the cart clattered its way up the rise to the steading, but the contents did not shift, luck was with the 'fermers'. Mercifully John decided to stop for a cup of tea before they had to unload, for which his wife was truly thankful. With the empty cart returned to its shed, Charlotte went inside to prepare food but the Kango battered the air for some time before John was content with the day.

All went according to the carefully measured plan with uprights concreted firmly in place ready to take lengths of tubing fastened together by the purchased clips. The areas railed off in front of the steading would be well-used in the winter to give cows and young stock firm footing and plenty of air without damaging sodden fields.

The first rectangle, gated in two places, was at its far end funnelled into narrow rails which led to the Monymusk gate and entrap-

149

ment. This specially strong crush gate was designed to hold an animal's head for as long as it took to make any examination or give treatment. For any such purpose space could be cut down by closing gates to give one-way traffic only. After release a cow would be enclosed as before in the second rectangular space – i.e. was tested or treated but still under control, awaiting others as they emerged from the crush. The system could be dismantled, gates and rails removed if necessary, but sufficient space remained in front of the steading for cars or tractors to pass. The space in front of the crush provided a layby. Like all John's schemes it was well thought out.

One big item remained. The whole area had to be concreted. John called in Mr Dees and his sons and arranged for Readymix concrete to be delivered. Many hands were needed to cope with this part of the operation, preparing the surface, dealing with the constant supply poured from the Readymix machine, spreading and levelling it, a labour of Hercules for one man to tackle. Charlotte kept the coffee pot at the ready and provided snacks, her easiest job for a long time. And so the whole thing was completed, the drying and hardening process merely a matter of time. Nobody could walk on the surfaces of course and any foray into the steading meant a detour round about. Land Rover and tractors were already parked strategically. Notices warned that there was no access.

No access for human beings or their wheels that is; pawprints were seen, it being easy to detect Tiger Tim's as he had extraordinarily big paddy-paws. There was also the gander's mark just at the edge nearest the Dutch barn, but he had not proceeded. Perhaps the feel of the stuff reminded him of the goose walks his forbears endured, their poor yellow feet tarred for the march to the London markets and certain destruction.

19

Aftermath

The barley was ready and John had notified Mr Dees, but the combine-harvester would not come until late morning. For the last few days the farm had been shrouded in haar which took time to clear. Early patrols came across phantom cattle which took familiar outline only when close enough for heads to lift at a quiet greeting, 'Well lassies, Well now!' Pheasants whirring into flight; the small thud of a rabbit hopping from its depredations; all other sound muted, plucked grass, the burn's ripple, the river itself flowing softly. Gorse bushes festooned with tiny beads of moisture, the deadened yellow flowers need the sun's light. The first leaves underfoot tell of autumn.

Tric-trac, Tric-trac ... the bridge signalled the heavy combine just after midday and harvesting began. Nothing for John to do as the silage pit was swept clear ready for a yield which looked reasonably heavy. A decision had been made to sell most of the barley because storing it in an old building was not ideal. As the fields were undersown all the straw would be useful as extra eating for the cattle later on. The aftermaths too would give a better bite for young stock moved there.

Until uplifted, any crop has predators to contend with: rats, pigeons, even small birds take to thieving and cats have something of a birthday. Before the barley ripened at Bithnie there were other trespassers: deer, herons, and also a couple of Frenchmen to be moved off. It appeared they had paid to shoot Forestry land but strayed to find easier game lower down, being elderly and averse to climbing. Whilst seeming to look askance at Charlotte's tattered jerkin, they had managed to summon Gallic charm and she could not resist offering them coffee. So crime was rewarded.

Meantime John got busy on a repair. The man digging the trench to house electric cable on one of his forays made savage impact into the garden wall so recently built. It could not be helped, there was very little room for manoeuvre and he had made apologies. Now the damage could be put right.

On a course organised by their friend from the Agricultural Training Board, John had learned about 'stane dykin'. A crumbling wall at Burnside provided the perfect site for the dozen or so learners to be shown how to tackle such a job. The master dyker, seventy years old, stocky and capable, knew all there was to know about his craft. He gave precise instructions. The very largest stones, lifted with care to avoid back strain, made a base for the wall. Smaller stones must be wedged in to fill any gaps leaving no space at all between these base stones. The wall should be built up gradually until, at the halfway point, long stones were put athwartships to tie in and compress those already in place. Again any gaps were to be filled in by small stones of appropriate shape. Further layers would complete the wall to the desired height. Finally, placed on edge, biggish stones, the headers, would top the wall and anchor it.

Those on the course were a mixed bunch: one or two farmers, several keen gardeners, the wife of a city councillor and one English lady with a very loud voice. Their reasons for attending might have been interesting. At any rate John benefited and from then on he was able to tackle many repairs about the farm. Always considered fit and strong, he had felt miffed when the old man brushed him aside as he was about to move a base stone.

'Nae laddie, leave that een. A'll dae that. Jis' leave it...' He had lifted the enormous stone as if it had been a piece of paper.

Representatives from the merchants came to inspect the barley and made their offers, the best of which was accepted. A cheque received was rather less than John calculated, the amount having deductions of various kinds in the buyer's favour but Charlotte sent it post-haste to gladden the Banker's heart, such benisons being few and far between. Outgoing sums were boosted however, as help was needed to load the sixteen-ton wagons which inched over the brig to collect the spoils.

Mr Dees had trundled his combine 'ower the brig' for the slow journey to another harvesting, leaving John waiting for the baler and praying that the fine weather would last; there was always a fear that it would not. Getting the straw off was the final task. He took a good look at the fence bordering the river and found one or two posts required supports – he had no desire to rescue swimmers when young stock grazed that park. He noticed a car pull into the layby and after a while saw two adults and two children carry rugs and picnic things to the riverbank. Later he saw that a fire had been lighted: it was to be full-scale cooking rather than sandwiches and lemonade. Aware of fire risk to straw ready for the baler he crossed the bridge to speak to the family. He sighed, expecting the sort of trespassers he crossed swords with now and again, but these people were from Bolivia, of all faraway places, and had only a smattering of English. With anxious smiles it was explained that they had made the fire very carefully, surrounding it with many stones, and they would douse it thoroughly when they left: truly there was no danger. In his former life John had met and got on particularly well with the Minister of Education in the Bolivian government of the day, and this had to be another case of 'hands across the sea'. They talked, making themselves understood somehow in a mixture of Spanish and English, with plenty of gestures thrown in. John was totally disarmed by the charm and good manners of the family.

'My wife will have something for your picnic,' he pointed to the house and the two children, 'if you will allow them?'

Charlotte was more than surprised to see John with two small companions chattering their way up the farm road. Having seen John go to the riverside she had expected a quick exodus of picnic party.

'This is Veronica and this is Rudi,' he introduced the two grave little people, who made quick bobs of acknowledgement at their names. Smiles soon appeared and helpless giggling as they attempted to communicate. Rudi was graphic in describing the holiday: he loved England and Scotland except for one thing, and this went, 'Bzz ... Bzz...' and was striped like his sister's T-shirt: he made stripes across his stomach and a violent pinging noise, the sting! He was very worried that he might get stung because he had 'allergia' and might die. He indicated how he would collapse. The eyes of his sister darkened in sympathy before both faces dissolved into mirth. Charlotte too was charmed. Out of the pantry came a sponge-cake and from the fridge, venison noisettes intended for supper: something else could be defrosted later on. Before the two trotted away down the road and back to the picnic, John made it clear that buzzing things with stripes never stung visitors to Bithnie Farm, especially the ones from Bolivia.

20

Metamorphosis

Walkers, hikers and ramblers, when they decided to take the various routes over his land, were a source of annoyance to John Grey. It would seem a simple thing to walk on a farm road, keep to a designated path, shut a gate, but it had not been the case. Trekking through corn or hayfields proved attractive, gates were left open, barbed wire

fences and stone walls offered the agile out-
doorsman a short cut. Jagged tins left in the
burn and silver foil retrieved from anywhere
on the farm, led to the conviction that
walkers, hikers and ramblers were of a
strange mentality, incapable of reading,
never mind following the Country Code.
There might be decent people who liked to
walk, but they went elsewhere, did not walk
towards Bithnie. The bother of pregnancy
testing young heifers and a vet's bill when
the bull had enjoyed a frolic through an
open gate smouldered in his memory and
no booted, bobble-hatted or haversacked
figure got a cheery welcome from John.
Some trespassers were defiant: 'Miserable
bugger!' floated back after he ejected a foot-
ball team from a park near the bridge.
Shortly afterwards he saw a smart car in the
same field and from it a man with a San
Tropez tan unloading fishing gear, seemingly prepared for a long stay. Probably this
discovery, in the wake of the wannabe
Beckhams caused the 'miserable bugger' to
give vent to language heard on destroyers,
not the official 'speak' of Her Majesty's
Navy but something infinitely more brutal.
John told Charlotte later that man had a
French accent, yet the entente cordiale did

not blossom: the car had upped anchor and steamed over the bridge at a rate of knots.

The time had come to separate Goldwater from the herd and for several days he was guided into the bull pen and fed there instead of with the cows in the steading. The ulterior motive was of course to fasten the gate on him when he was thoroughly used to isolation and all the comforts provided – ample hay of best quality, a specially arranged sleeping area, a water trough with no queues. John had seen bulls kept in all conditions and some were not housed well, one in particular in a dark, damp place without room enough to turn round. This Simmental bull was permanently in a rage, the farm man afraid of him. Not a good prospect for the Bithnie herd, a chain rattling hate when John and the orraman approached. Seeing that a sale was unlikely the man volunteered, 'Naeb'dy wints yon bugger. Ah reckon the boss'll ha te pit 'im doon the road.'

'That would be a mercy after the way you keep him!'

It was no use blaming the old man, but the 'boss' got an opinion he did not like, together with a threat of the SSPCA. But really it was too late, too late for the poor beast who had

159

probably been mistreated from birth. It was enough to turn the stomach – ignorance, carelessness or blind cruelty, whatever name you gave it.

Goldwater was more fortunate, the pen light and airy, with a walled-off sleeping place where a daily addition of fresh straw would give a deep warm bed. A strong gate from Monymusk ensured cleaning and strawing out involved no risk. Brimful of food, a bull was only too ready to lie down and at the time would hardly notice being shut off. Standing at the front of the pen gave a view of all that was going on about the farm and some sort of contact with his cows. Their soft noses could reach to him through the bars. In due course Goldwater became a focus of interest to all visitors: 'Hey, min!' or 'Fit like laddie?' or 'Foo's yersel big boy?' Postie and others calling out to him were rewarded by a steady gaze from the honest face sought and found. He was not averse to a scratch behind the ears. Regarding bulls in general Charlotte had gone from petrifying fear and apprehension of the first ones on Burnside to a great pride in Goldwater. Perched on the outer gate she groomed him regularly, brushing and combing free of knots the thick curls on his noble head. Seeing the care lavished on the quiescent bull made John think of Burnside and a gathering dusk when to his horror she leapt to separate Angus bulls having a fight! Twenty-four hours earlier she had been unwilling to go anywhere near a bull! He had been very very angry at the time, Charlotte as *torero* way beyond his comprehension but then women ... enigma! The present beauty treatment reminded him to check the sugar beet nuts: he strongly suspected they were raided for Goldwater.

All calm at Bithnie. A spell of fair weather allowed painting to go ahead on the steading. The four enormous doors were darkened to blend more easily with the green of the brae. The general appearance of the farm was improved, the new concrete kept clean by using a power washer bought for the purpose. Using this machine was to Charlotte like housework made enjoyable, being in the open air. It was good to direct fierce jets to dissolve the ever-present sharn and send it swirling away down the drains leaving a pristine expanse. There was something else: the name, power washer! In the hand, power ... oblique approach towards other green wellies, the hose allowed to slip just enough to give a wholesome shower. If you managed not to laugh you could quickly call out 'Sorry!' but only once. People could end up ridiculously wet.

Patrols round the stock were enjoyable, the herd looking bonny, calves sleek and well fed, the yearlings thriving. It seemed that for once they could relax. An interesting chance to do so came from a friend of a friend with an invitation to visit an oil rig. The sea after so long on dry land, a helicopter journey, the process of oil extraction and its machinery – irresistible. Not for Charlotte: the idea of landing on a tiny platform in the middle of the wild North Sea held no appeal and her polite refusal masked an Eliza Dolittle's 'Not bloody likely!' It took time to arrange the outing with Jerry, the American who had business on the rig. Before any date was fixed there came a telephone call, a female voice, low and somehow lilting:

'Do ah heave the Bithnie Faarm?' And on an affirmative, 'Ah would laike te speak with Mr Greay if he is theeyar?'

Mr Grey was not but the message was clear. 'Ah need te knaow haow tawall Mr Greay is, and the sayize of his feet, ASAP if you cayen!'

Charlotte took down the number and promised to ring. 'Well whaddaye knaow!' she couldn't wait to pass the message on.

'Do admit, John. It is nice for a change.'

She had on her best dress and good shoes. John in a carefully preserved Chester Barry suit gave a reluctant 'Mmm!'

Really, he felt constrained, not himself, and this skylark was a waste of time when all you could possibly want was on the farm. The Land Rover rattled the bridge but on the main road came to a stop. Two elderly ladies looked hopeful as Charlotte wound down her window, their car tilted into a ditch behind them. It took only seconds for John to rummage in the back of the Land Rover for a rope. The ladies, elegant in lace, were genteel moths around the shining knight. Charlotte with set face waited. Granted that being a problem solver was brilliant, why did he have to leap into action this evening? Just for once why not leave it to somebody else? She would be more than annoyed if Sir Galahad got oil on his shirt.

'Full ahead!' The rather ancient vehicle was eased back onto the road and soon underway.

'Funny that,' John volunteered, 'they're off to Gavin's dressed to the nines like us.'

It was Charlotte's turn for a noncommittal 'Mmm...'

Something of a socialite, though a farmer, Gavin had asked anyone and everyone to a soirée with music. He and his family were at the door to welcome and usher people inside where two adjoining rooms gave space for rows of chairs facing an improvised stage. The two ladies fluttered back to say how glad they were not to have made John and Charlotte late.

A considerable buzz dwindled when Gavin stepped on the stage. Full of bonhomie and perhaps a little of the water of life, he asked for applause for a well-known violinist and a cellist, but named the viola player as the wife of the wrong one. It did not matter. It was going to be good, the time of year, the right ambience, the Howe *en fête*.

Briefly Mozart then Dohnanyi, strange and unfamiliar but interesting, then Gavin again saying, 'Wine and food everybody!' In effect, my house is yours. Red wine and white and dollops of this and that. A rising flood of talk to friends, neighbours, strangers; Charlotte glad she bounced John into accepting the invitation. The warm old house, the company, like an old painting come to life...

Gavin, the rubicund host enjoying himself tremendously. Instruments laid aside while the musicians mingled. Postie, doctor, grander people from somewhere. Farmers old and young, wives and girlfriends. More often than not Radio 1 belted out from their tractors, but nae matter, this was fine. The violinist happy to discuss music and Charlotte mentioning her niece, a harpist well-paid for playing at the swish London hotels. Yes, all the rage at the moment for young women. Charlotte admitting Victoria was young and also beautiful and his graceful, 'She would be!' as he moved on. Comment from John about smooth so-and-sos fading into 'Oh my God!' on catching sight of Gavin, his hand on the shoulder of a tall man with a wonderfully tanned face. John with a sudden need to beam up the smaller moth for deep conversation. Genial Gavin introducing the bronzed hulk, hand-kissing, faces suffused with pleasure, but not the men's. A flittering moth-lady and then Charlotte:

'My dear, I want you to meet Francois, one of my oldest friends.'

As if in a dream a hand taken, skimmed in salute, eyes of unbelievable depth twinkling down. *Et voilà!* The third moth! Faintly then, detaching John from his acolyte:

165

'Monsieur Francois, my husband, John Grey.'

John, with stiff upper lip, 'We have met I believe...'

'Ah yes, I theenk so, but you were perhaps in a great hurry, *n'est ce pas?*' Entente at last.

More talk and more music. Sincere thanks to Gavin for a wonderful evening and they were on the way home. At first silent against the thump of the diesel, John summoned his thoughts.

'I think it's bloody marvellous how they turn into princes,' he said.

21

Trauchled

When early feeding of the stock began in the autumn, the calves had access to an area of the steading separate from the cows. Quickly they learned that by going through a gate which had one space wide enough for a small body to pass through they could get at food without being pushed out of the way by their betters. It was interesting to see even the smallest and youngest calf get the idea and become confident enough to leave 'mum' for the bonus of the best hay and a 'puckle' of calf nuts. The 'creep' gate made weaning a much simpler affair: gone were the days when separation took time and much chasing of wily bodies determined to stick to a milk diet. When the opening was blocked by the addition of a sturdy iron bar there was uproar, anguished blaring of separated mother and child, frantic efforts to break through, yielding to despair and dismal croaking as voices failed. Charlotte hated this necessary process, could hardly bear to watch the more devoted cows seeking even after days of separation to nuzzle their offspring through the bars of the gate. When John seemed to be occupied elsewhere she was guilty of dipping into the expensive concentrates in an attempt to comfort. Aware of the depredations he made no comment, being a merciful man.

When 'the tumult and the shouting died' there was nothing for it but to arrange the next item on the farming calendar, the annual test to ensure herds remained free from the scourge of brucellosis and this was combined with testing for tuberculosis. Like all disagreeable operations the test loomed over them long before an actual date was fixed: it had to be taken into account in many ways – for instance, in the movement of the herd to fresh pasture when grass close to the steading had to be kept for the vital day. Any thought of the test made the heart sink, as so much could go wrong. One year Irene earned the reputation of 'dyke-lowper' by launching herself to clear first one then a second gate, leaving the metal bars considerably bowed at the top. Shock effect, helpers galvanised into action, cattle in a stir, vet with syringe poised unable to continue. Luckily she was undamaged but getting blood from her afterwards was a problem; isolated and left to the very last minute she was still trembling and wild-eyed, almost on the point of collapse. Great patience was needed before that test came to an end with sandwiches in the farm kitchen and the usual benison from the water of life.

During any test there is risk: a beast's leg caught between metal bars is in danger of snapping; kicks lashed out in panic find a target; hands get trapped; a bruise colours up and a swelling appears. Elimination of disease is the purpose but this fails to register at the time of battle. When the final blood sample is taken and the captives are released, relief is the overwhelming emotion. Year after year at Burnside the diary recorded trauma, and sometimes read, 'We are drained and exhausted'.

Remembered hazards cast long shadows at Bithnie before telephone calls were made to the vet to fix a date and to people who were likely to help on the day of the test. Previously the farm had produced cereal crops or hay with sheep grazing the braes. Now the cattle had no contact at all with others, there were no adjoining parks with grazing animals, the river being another isolating factor. So rather than fear of the wrong result of a test it was in Scottish terms, the tyauve, the stramash, that worried Charlotte and John. It was also a test of their own stamina; they would have to 'grin and bear it' year after year and that was not a pretty thought.

They set about the preparation. Courts strawed out, big round bales dropped by tractor into the circular feeders used in place of the high troughs. At the start the cows could munch away, unaware of vet and hypodermic. *En route* from the grazing to the bribes laid out in the steading every possible diversion was eliminated and the way made straight and narrow. When the time came someone would shut the gate so there was no going back.

The concrete area in front of the steading would be available at first but as soon as the vet arrived the tall steading doors could be closed and the herd contained in the court. Was anything forgotten? Telephone calls to Dugald, Gil and others to remind them? No need to ring the vet. An attempt to relax over the evening meal and an early bed. It was St Crispin's Eve.

The blessing of a fine morning and John went to collect the herd, singling out Lucy to bring the other cows from the braes. A gentle amble down the slope was spoiled: the newcomer forgot that the noise of a car and a stranger approaching was enough to make the cows turn hastily back from whence they came. It could not be helped but it was a bad start.

After the vet arrived a few cows were released from the steading and the doors shut tight again. With varying degrees of hassle these were funnelled one by one into the race and to prevent them backing out from there it was Charlotte's job to insert a heavy metal pole behind each one. As the animal moved forward towards the crush and another followed, the poles had to be placed behind them, one animal, one pole, and it had to be quick. Finally in the crush the head was trapped and held sideways by John while the vet drew blood from a vein in the neck. The details of each cow were marked on the tube receiving the sample. Some cows struggled dangerously within the confines of the crush and would not put their heads forward to be trapped. Others simply refused to go into the crush, so that someone pretty athletic had to climb aloft, using both feet to propel the broad body along. It was tiring and risky doing this. One or two cows reared up and came down with feet hanging over the top rail of the en-closure, or between the lower bars. A broken needle caused delay, as did an incorrect identification of very similar bodies. There was much frustration and there was a great deal of sharn. Tails were lifted all too often and strangely the process could be repeated almost immediately. People slipped and were shat upon. There was a lot of language. It has to be remarked that in the midst of all the turmoil Goldwater behaved like a gent, mak-ing not a murmur about giving his blood. After nearly four hours of blood, sweat and other substances, it was over for another year.

22

Sales

After the test there followed an interval, a pause when apart from ensuring the herd had hay to supplement the waning quality of the grazing, they did little else, made no onslaught on things remaining on their list. It was a sort of Indian summer for them, time to take a breather, to look back on what had been achieved rather than attempt anything further: they looked after the cattle, and that was all. For once a trip to Aberdeen did not have to be a rushed and desperate affair to get supplies for house and farm, call on the civil servants at Gallowgate or the tax man. The objective was a simple one – Charlotte wanted some new shoes.

Postie arrived as they were setting out and brought amongst the bills a letter from Lisa which Charlotte opened as the Land Rover rattled over the bridge:

Darling Charlotte

I think your ears must be permanently on fire just now. I have been lamenting your absence more than ever because I am dreadfully in Mike's bad books. All to do with shopping. He seems to have the idea that when we shopped together in the old days you curbed me! Did you? I do not remember. Well, it started when I went to a sale, not the ordinary kind but at Tyrrels, they were closing down temporarily for a total refurbish and honestly darling they were giving things away! I bought a few oddments and then I saw a bedspread, perfect for our giant bed and I won't bore you except to tell it is palest cream jacquard with a lovely scalloped edge and oodles of discount. I also picked up four pillowcases to match. At least I thought so but showing them to Mike found two of them were straight edged, no scallops. I kept them anyway because changing things is such a bother but went back and easily found two more scalloped ones so that was all right. Except when I got home I found one was for a square pillow. Perhaps I should have stopped there but the sale was still on and I went back to get the right sort of scallopy normal size and thought 'Oh what the heck' and bought a pillow to fit the square and not waste it. It was the very last week with stupendous bargains but I was determined to be careful and the only things I added were six towels for the guest bathroom. Mike had been just the teeniest bit cross before but the last straw was the towels, such a super shade of green, turning out to be *bathmats*.

At the moment we are not speaking.

How are you both? Write soon.

Much love, Lisa

'The usual stuff from Lisa?' asked John as they walked from the car park. 'Mike all right?'

'A bit off, actually. You must read it later.'

John's patience was wearing thin. It seemed to him that every shoe in Aberdeen had been tried and rejected for no reason at all and the present port of call had an expensive feel about it, a lot of space with leather chairs and a hushed atmosphere. Gliding rather than walking over lush pile, elegant figures went to and fro wearing the sort of shoes they sold. Customers were shown deference at the same time as a certain disdain: in pale, manicured hands every shoe became a votive offering. The model girl who prowled towards Charlotte was tall and pencil-slim. Hardly disturbing the smoothness of her perfect make-up she allowed a smile to rest briefly on Charlotte and a fraction of a second longer on John. After a while she brought temptation in soft green leather with a heel higher than Charlotte usually wore.

'The Italians,' breathed the goddess, 'they have no equal! These are perfect, quite perfect on you modom!'

The low voice had the diction of a Kirsty Wark and the certainty, but Charlotte took off the green shoes and chose navy blue court shoes.

Back at the farm John was curious. 'I thought the green ones were nice,' he said.

'I *was* tempted,' Charlotte admitted. She rummaged in her handbag to find Lisa's letter and handed it over. She watched him read it, saw the shake of his head as he thought, 'Women!' She was unpacking what they had bought. A man would never see that shoes like that, at such a price, and the colour so subtle, needed everything: dress, suit or even a coat, all new, the total ensemble, and all beyond her pocket. It was bloody sometimes having to be so canny with money but there it was.

John handed back the letter, grinning at

her. 'I believe Cinders thought the green shoes might turn into wellies when she got 'em home!'

He ducked and the kippers intended for supper missed by a mile. Blackie rescued them swiftly and managed not to choke on the bones.

23

Comin's an' goin's

Shortly after the shoe hunting day in Aberdeen John and Charlotte went to Burnside to visit the family there. It was good to see them happy and enthusiastic about their plan to build another house using the pink granite of the former steading. Lochnagar would be in view from the main rooms...

Full many a glorious morning have I seen
Flatter the mountain tops with sovereign eye,
Kissing with golden face the meadows green,
Gilding pale streams with wondrous alchemy...

there to be seen on the 'bonny days' and all the other days.

John saw that the dining room of the new house would be roughly where in the old stable Gertie had sent him 'erse ower tip' when he was trying to treat her calf for 'scoor'.

Margaret and John had given up their handsome Aberdeen house in a similar way to John and Charlotte leaving the old house in England. Probably friends had reacted with the same disbelief that anyone would want to live at the 'back of beyond'. Those people could not know that the back of beyond had a magic of its own and the new owners of Burnside would be quick to find it. A surprising candour was there also: John W., retired from his profession of consultant gynaecologist, was well-known and greatly respected throughout Aberdeenshire and beyond. A chap working on the farm had cut his hand and of course John attended to it. Surveying the bandage rapidly becoming less than pristine as he touched it, the patient gave his opinion, 'By God A'michty! Ye surely arra roch bugger!'

Sheep were the main enterprise but they had also bought Angus cows, hardy black beauties ideal for the high farm. Progeny from the native breed had lost favour in the eyes of most farmers and yet it was admitted they produced the finest beef. Strange and perverse to put the giant Charolais to the little Angus cow, to risk health and longevity for the sake of extra size. Extra taste the Continental breed certainly did not provide: pink, dense in texture, lacking veining to keep the beef moist when cooking, it was the current fad, and should not last. At least that was what John dared to hope.

Dugald was amused by Charlotte's idea of life down under.

'Were they really like in films and TV ads?' she wanted to know. 'Drinking a lot of beer from cans and talking about motor-bikes and sheilas?' Dugald admitted it was a fairly accurate picture.

'I gather they can lift a sheep with one hand, shear it in seconds and reach for another!'

'Minutes, not seconds,' said Dugald, laughing.

Adapt or perish says the sage. Somewhat in the mould of the empire builders of other days, steadfast, upright, passionately attached to home and family but determined to cope, Dugald had adapted. It must have delighted John and Margaret to get him home, and home was now Burnside.

Dugald had been burning gorse and his cows were relishing the result: foraging the scorched earth yielded tastes beyond imagining. Dusty black faces lifted as John and Charlotte passed. The effect on the creamy-white of Hereford-Shorthorns had been bolder, made commandos of them, an army ranging the land, hard to recognise one from another.

It was a pleasure to walk on the hill again; the brown earth and slippery tight-grazed grass, the little streams, moorhens on a quiet pool, every path, every stone familiar. In winter when the world was white for miles and miles around Charlotte was photographed on the hill like Pilgrim walking forth into the wilderness. Their very first calf had come 'erse fust' into the world by the wavery light of a lantern and the aid of a well-thumbed textbook while a fearsome blizzard raged. The same hill, but this time white with a plethora of windflowers stirred by gentle breezes. Fencing where an alien bull had broken through to fight, turning their 'quiet bull' into a raging warrior and Charlotte into *torero*. John trekking to discuss the broken fence only to be vanquished by Hannah

Grace. Calvings in the quiet hours; a mother's frantic licking at betraying birth fluids; the damp strip of a tail quivering delight at the first suck of milk. And always the pure air and a backdrop of the distant mountain. The hill teemed with memories for John and Charlotte, a place where they had seen all things, good and bad, and somehow survived.

Tric-trac ... tric-trac ... the Fowlers visited. As the first people involved in John and Charlotte's search for a farm they continued to be interested in 'the Bithnie folk' as they were now described. At table in the kitchen someone would say: 'Ah, how the time has flown,' and they would recall how they happened to meet.

John and Charlotte had driven from Mersea Island fully intending to make the journey in two stages, staying the night somewhere *en route*. But the Alfa-Romeo, that 'red streak' had done so well that Newcastle, the border, Jedburgh and Lauder were behind them and Edinburgh was ahead. Speeding traffic there made it too complicated to look for somewhere to stay, so on they went, Aberdeen next. Again the bewilderment of a strange city at night, the lights, one-way streets. Their planned route was useless. No time to check the map but Charlotte saw 'Alford Road' signposted. Alford was the place they were heading for, so a hotel along here would be perfect. There was no hotel on the Alford road, or at least they did not see one. And now they were streaking out of town, green fields and sheep and sleeping cattle showing in the car lights. Hardly anyone else on the road, more fields, clusters of new houses, a pub or two, unlit... Tiredness and a sinking feeling, not from hunger alone though brief stops for a bite and drink of thermos tea seemed an age ago. They had not expected this! Eyes probing the darkness ... nothing ... a gap, was that a signpost? The words 'Bed & B'fast' blanked off. Worth a try? Charlotte staggered out of the car, an uneven road to a farmhouse but knocking at the door eventually produced, 'No! We're nae open, jist the summer months,' from a woman anxious to shut the door.

'Is Alford far off? Will we get a hotel there?'

'I dinnae think it, there's nae hotel I mind.'

What cheer to take back to John.

Ever onwards. Villages, sparse of lights, people there not late to bed. Further miles and another blanked-off sign, another try, and it was Mrs Fowler answering Charlotte, who had taken a few miles too many and was without hope.

'Ah, but we're closed jist noo.'

'I feared so! Will there be somewhere in Alford, do you think? A hotel there?' An involuntary catch in the voice of the traveller.

'I dinnae think it.'

Charlotte afterwards claimed that like taking in a stray cat, Mrs F took pity on the bedraggled waif at her door and made an offer: 'If ye help me mak' up the bed?'

A bite to eat in a warm kitchen and friendliness as well as a comfortable bed. John Fowler's accent baffled them but this quiet, pleasant-looking man had been a farmer and was able to tell them about the place they had come to see, a farm called Broomhill. They had known the owner was a Member of Parliament at Westminster, but were unaware of a partner who saw to the working of the place.

'Does he live there? The partner?'

'No. They hiv a grieve i'the hoose, looks efter the beasts ye ken. Bit ah nivver heeard a whisper aboot sellin'!'

'There's nae spik aboot it!' his wife agreed.

John showed them the relevant papers.

'Weel, weel, richt eneuch!'

They offered all they knew, a mine of information in fact, about Broomhill, where it was and how to get to it, from Leggerdale, that it was a good farm. The MP was a decent man and had a son who probably did not want to farm. The partner they did not know but rumour said he had a rich wife. From John Grey, 'That's exactly what I need, but I have a problem...'

'Nae a'b'dy's sae lucky!'

The owner was a charming, civilised man who explained his need to sell as he showed them around. They told him of their plans and he seemed to accept totally that John would become a farmer, but like Mrs Fowler he obviously wondered about Charlotte.

'It would be very strange for you, Mrs Grey, I think, giving up your life in England for...' He waved in the direction of the tiny farmhouse.

Mrs Fowler had said gravely to Charlotte, 'It's a hard life if ye're nae accustomed...'

Charlotte later put it in the vernacular: 'They were not just clicking the teeth!'

Swallowing all doubts, particularly about one room in the house crammed with mysterious rubbish, they had determined to bid for the farm. They became excited at the prospect and back on Mersea Island kept in touch with the Fowlers, the Doric more difficult than ever on the telephone. The closing date for bids was in late December. In preparation John decided to go to Smithfield Show, the most important livestock show of the year. He paid the entrance fee, walked into the hall and there of all people was the owner of Broomhill! Coincidence? Omen?

To a tentative hope that the sale would go well and in John's favour came a non-committal reply: 'There has been a good deal of interest!'

It produced a niggling doubt. Had their offer been on the low side? Had other people offered a good deal more? After discussion with Charlotte John decided to increase the bid. And waited, waited for the short December days to pass... It was no good: the partner became the owner of the whole farm. You had to recognise this solution was the likely one. A clear indication of the value had been gained by advertising the farm for sale. For Charlotte the smallest of consolations was the thought of the grieve's spare room.

Mr Ross, a newsagent who lodged at Leggerdale, sent on the weekly farming edition of the *Aberdeen Press & Journal* and eventually there appeared an advertisement for Burnside. John was off the mark, alone this time, by air to Aberdeen to hire a car and inspect not only that farm but two others. That he chose Burnside is of course history.

On any journey to Aberdeen John would give a toot on the horn passing Leggerdale, indicating that they would pay a quick call on the way back. Often that quick call lengthened into taking tea and something Mrs Fowler had made – oatcakes, scones, cake. Always the welcome was there, and a general 'newsing' on what was happening on the farms nearby and talk of cattle sales, or 'roups', if anyone was retiring and therefore disposing of good stock. Politics came under discussion with a healthy distrust of the ways of politicians. By now Charlotte had allayed fears that she would not adapt to the farming life, and John gained approval because he tackled anything and everything that cropped up, unafraid to 'rowe up his sark sleeves'. It was something of a relief that the idea of the 'rich fowk frae Lunnon' never found credence at Leggerdale. John and Charlotte were accepted as people anxious to make a success of their venture and could not have received more support. The guardian angel had done well in pointing Charlotte in the direction of that house.

There was humour always. On one visit a young man was present when John and Charlotte were at odds over something in the news involving women's rights. Charlotte put forward a strong condemnation of the man in the case. Euan, aged about seventeen, had listened carefully before remarking to John, 'Ye ken, yon lassie's oot o' control!'

It had to be said that the 'lassie' was old enough to be his mother.

They had first talked to Stuart at Burnside where he had been accustomed to shoot before they owned the farm.

Aware of the local way of things John had invited him back to the house to take 'a dram' but Stuart had not accepted.

'I am away to see ma wife, Heather, who has jist presented me with a son and heir!'

This son and heir, tucked up in the maternity wing of an Aberdeen hospital, slept unaware that he was to be named Andrew Charles Stuart and was the owner of an expensive rifle bought to celebrate him. That sort of birthday present was out of Charlotte's experience but she made no comment. It was early days in what was to become a solid, valued friendship.

Stuart became intrigued by the idea of buying land. When a Burnside neighbour decided to retire, he put his farm up for sale and Stuart went to see it with Heather, then heavily pregnant with their second child. They took Gin, a King Charles spaniel, a well-trained small dog who needed exercise and was unlikely to upset farm animals. The brightness of an early morning faltered and vanished with a plunging temperature. Rising wind, and a splattering of snow became blizzard, sharp and stinging. So, toiling back to Burnside they came, Stuart, Heather and the little dog. Ambulant snow shapes, two people with a *Magic Roundabout* eskimo-dog arrowing alongside. Even in the warm kitchen the Inuit took a long time to thaw. Unfortunately their bid for the land was unsuccessful. Still, as Scarlett said in the film, 'Tomorrow is another day.' Stuart eventually bought the farm at one time the focus of a long, long journey from Essex and an unsuccessful bid by John and Charlotte.

Now and again Heather brought the children to see Charlotte. Andrew did not like getting out of the car onto the road in front of the steading.

'Dis John like all this mud?'

'Well, not really Andrew. He will get it concreted as soon as he can.'

Heather Lynne Joy, or 'Little Heather', starting school and somehow at odds with the teacher, unburdened herself to Charlotte on a later visit. She was grumbled at or punished, often for talking in class: she did try not to, though the work was very hard. Heavy lashes blinked away tears, a deep sigh and resignation on the charming small face.

'I s'pose I'll jist hev to put up with it!'

Charlotte restrained a desire to throttle a well-respected local teacher.

Later still there was a sister for Andrew and Heather. Charlotte inspected the very new little being asleep in one of the latest carry-cot affairs. A tiny perfect face peeped above a pale coverlet.

'She had a touch of jaundice,' Heather explained, pointing to a mere tinge of colour on the delicate skin.

'She is lovely, absolutely lovely,' Charlotte avowed. 'She reminds me of something, a little rose, a rosebud...' Not a reference to the classic film *Citizen Kane*, nothing except the impression of something carefully protected, just beginning. The bud was named Fiona Carole Ann. Nevertheless on Christmas cards, letters or telephone messages from

Bithnie or anywhere else Stuart, Heather, Andrew, Little Heather and Rosebud were named. Charlotte was careful never to ask what Fiona Carole Ann thought of that.

When the Land Rover needed attention from Mr Smith at the garage, Stuart was quick to offer the use of one of his vehicles, a Lada pick-up. John had arrived at the garage in farm clothes and wellington boots, size eleven. After a chat he made his way over to Stuart and Heather's house where the Lada waited, ready for action. The drive sloped towards the main road and large boots are not the best thing when a small car's pedals are close together: braking was less than effective. However, there was no traffic or witness to this fairly explosive start. But the problem did not go away. A slight touch on the accelerator seemed to produce an unwarrantable surge of power and Bigfoot could not find the delicate touch necessary to drive the vehicle when half his boot accelerated and the other half braked. Somehow he achieved top gear and made progress, fast, as was the norm for John. Crossroads ahead where three or four men were digging a trench and a change of gear was desirable to turn right. Belting on at thirty miles per hour, no way was this possible for the wellie boots. Fifty yards from the turning. Fifty yards from the trench. Fifty yards from workmen aghast that the local pharmacist hurtling towards them had no intention of slowing down. No time to ponder the mystery. Better to leap into the embrace of a thorny hedge. A screeching turn; easy to guess what was going on behind but no look in the mirror to confirm as the famed 'Brig of Alford' loomed, narrow, room only for one vehicle at a time. John managed to slow a little but could not stop: a guardian angel delayed oncoming traffic. And so on to the next hazard, the hairpin bend for home. Guardian angel still on duty for the perilous turn onto the Bithnie brig, tric-trac, tric-trac, the stout planks slowing him for the steep farm road and a shuddering stop outside the bull pen, Goldwater's handsome head querying over the gate. Neat whisky from a puzzled Charlotte and the comfort of a cat who settled on his lap as he drank it. Bigfoot was home and dry-ish.

24

Sheeters

'The trouble about rabbits is...'

'...they breed like rabbits!' John finished the sentence for Charlotte. He knew she disliked the idea of shooting anything but it had to be faced: the small creature of the story books, the denizen of the hutch in the garden, furry substitute for a more demanding pet, was an absolute menace on the farm. And her cats loved rabbit meat, rated it higher than tinned food. He told people, 'Not pheasants', although he himself enjoyed it cooked the French way with cream and apples.

Charlotte had to concede that action must be taken to stop a rabbit takeover, so Alan and Donald, or Angus and Abby would end up sampling a late breakfast after trekking the length and breadth of the farm, ruddy still from the keen air. At John's suggestion they would leave the spoils out of sight, though in Charlotte's mind the sorry piles existed whether she saw them or not.

Charlotte would leave the steading early to get the big breakfast under way. Sausages, bacon, eggs, tomatoes, fried bread, masses of toast, butter, all to vanish like snow in summer. The Aga was a boon though, simplicity itself when it came to putting food on the table, as well as giving the comfort of a warm kitchen. Sometimes you needed that in the sort of summer you got in Scotland, but the autumn days could be lovely, crisp and dry, with a benign quality of light over everything, making the farm a very pleasant place to be.

Charlotte tried to get the timing right, wanting to have things piping hot for the shooters' return, but she could only guess. They would come back when the job was done. Often there were interruptions, other things to see to, perhaps callers or the telephone ringing or to feed Tiger who always came in late, his anxious face peering round the door to make sure Blackie was not about. With strange people in the house he would vanish: none of the cats could cope with that. She would probably find them under the bed, hostilities suspended until the aliens were away down the road. If she allowed herself to think of the poor dead bunnies she would probably crawl under there with them.

On one occasion a distant relative of Stuart's came with a shooting party and when he stepped inside the house and removed his cap a shock of red-gold hair beautifully complemented the dull green of his coat. Charlotte was immediately reminded of the poem by Yeats but mentioning this to John afterwards met with alarm.

'You didn't say anything? Quote at him?'

She could not resist. 'Of course! Whyever not?' And in a sonorous voice, 'I heard an old religious man but yesternight declare, that he had found a text to prove that only God, my dear, could love you for yourself alone and not your yellow hair!'

'You must have frightened the life...'

She was trying not to laugh. 'Well, I nearly did! And if he comes again...'

On the other farm Angus and Abby helped tackle the problem of rabbits and once Abby brought a ferret. The result had been unexpected. They had arrived early, travelling from Bucksburn, the ferret's neat little box in the boot of the car alongside a shotgun and a rifle which Abby, an expert shot, would use. John had been rather taken with the ferret, creamy-gold in colour, its beady eyes and twitching whiskers so alert, the sinuous body quick to disappear into Abby's deep pocket. The ferret's name was Fred, and Fred was to be a major weapon in the war. They walked to a spot where John feared the rabbits were establishing a commune. He wondered whether the Japanese had got their idea of capsule hotels from rabbits.

'Ah'll leave the futtrat with the twa o'ye an' tak' a look roond masel.' Abby put the ferret down a hole before walking purposefully towards the hill, the rifle at his shoulder, an empty canvas bag on his back. John with his rifle and Angus with the shotgun took up stations a few yards away, ready for action.

Very soon a rabbit popped a head outside.

'Crack!' and 'Bang!' went the weapons but the head vanished before the projectiles reached it.

Again, again, and yet again! The same thing! They persevered. Heads popped out, guns fired, heads disappeared. They were not making progress.

And then realisation. In dismay they looked at each other.

'God A'michty!' said Angus.

'Fred!' said John.

How could Abby be told their rabbits had all been Fred? They held fire. Perhaps a real rabbit would come out if they waited long enough. After a time a head did come out but it was Fred again. Fred, suffering and unable to trust daylight, retreating into the blanket of the dark, with the rabbits. Post-traumatic stress disorder might describe the state he was in. Or as Angus muttered, 'He's bloody terrified John!'

'Thinks we hate him,' agreed John, 'and how are we going to tell Abby...'

'...his ferret needs psychiatric treatment!' Angus caught sight of Abby returning. He was weighted down to the gunwales, as John put it, his belt festooned all around with corpses, the bag obviously very heavy.

'How d'ye git on?' he asked.

Confession and an ignominious retreat to the farmhouse where breakfast was waiting.

Fred came out at once when Abby called his name and rapidly insinuated himself into the haven of the deep pocket. If ferrets do pray, he was undoubtedly praying to stay away from Burnside, for ever and ever.

25

Fechters

Long ago in that previous life newspapers had carried a paragraph about John head-lined, 'Britain's only bearded judge and ref-eree leaves...' Somewhat of an exaggeration, but the leaving part was correct. It was hinted that he would continue with the Amateur Boxing Association in Scotland but in truth John knew he was going to be too busy with his cows to do judging or anything else. He was developing a sort of tunnel vision of the life to come and surprised even Charlotte with the amount of effort he put into research. A day or two before their move an odd encounter took place. John came across a boxing crony and they talked for a while before what John thought was goodbye.

'See you tonight!' said Les.

'What?' from a puzzled bearded judge.

'At the do, your presentation!'

It had been arranged, the presentation of a

silver tankard, bearing an engraved message reading, 'To John Grey esquire from his friends in the Amateur Boxing Association'. The trouble was they'd forgotten to tell him!

Many, many moons later John was one of a party of people from the Howe going to watch boxing arranged by the Scottish branch of the ABA. They left the village, vet, pharmacist, banker, butcher, farmer and others in a hired minibus driven by a local man keen on the sport. It was to be a formal, dressed-up kind of 'do', with kilts and the supporting gear, and one man ventured a decidedly avant-garde purple jacket. At Stuart's house before leaving, John had been persuaded to try on a kilt belonging to Stuart and was photographed wearing it and a surprised expression. It goes without saying that he kept to his sober dinner jacket, which luckily still fitted.

The minibus trundled along towards the granite city, the road quietish after the day's traffic. Past Tillyfourie, past Leggerdale where John Fowler and his wife would have settled to the television. On through the extended sprawl of Westhill and eventually to a hotel near the airport. A lounge like every other hotel lounge thickly carpeted and containing a bar which John aproached with the idea of ordering drinks. He was stopped by a smiling Stuart.

'Aa's seen to!'

And seen to it was, with bottles of malt whisky and other liquids on every one of the party's reserved tables. Drouth would not hinder concentration on the boxing.

Opinions are sharply contrasted about the sport. Some have the idea that it is brutal and dangerous, and professional boxers have scars to show, but as an amateur affair, under strict rules, many of the objections fail and in their place are suggestions of a more positive effect: a young man in training does not smoke, or drink to excess and is most unlikely to take drugs. At the gym or slogging away at roadwork in order to be in peak condition for a fight requires discipline. A coloured word, fight, a red rag to a bull, but more than ever nowadays a controlled ability to defend oneself does not come amiss. John had worked with a Commander Lawrence who taught his own boy to box before sending him away to school and found that boys in his village were eager to join the sessions. After a time a flourishing network of clubs had spread through the county and the police gave support.

'You've helped keep a lot of lads off the

street,' the Commander was told.

The programme unfolded with good bouts and less good: courage and timidity, inexperience and confidence took turns in the ring. Liquid levels in all bottles lowered in proportion to rising appreciation, sympathy or disapproval. Unflagging effort, grunts of expelled air as arms jab and heads weave from side to side. Sportsmanship shown by victor and vanquished alike.

And so it came to an end, the minibus at the door, but it was a long time before the men of the Howe assembled and still one seat lacked a body. Haphazard search and eventual discovery on one of the hotel's generous sofas, out to the world or as a not too sober gentleman observed, 'Pisshed oota 'is mind.'

'Legless' was another way of putting it as four unsteady comrades with some difficulty lifted him from the imitation leather.

At odd times and in unusual circumstances one of the party was apt to burst into song and did so now when progress was less than rapid. 'Fou-r corners to-oo my bed...' and in crescendo, 'fi-i-ive ange-e-hells there be-hee spread, two-hoo at my head, two-hoo at my fee-heet.' He was struck by the cleverness of his choice of song but was unable to continue, having forgotten where the fifth angel went and none of the Scots could help out; funny that!

The journey home was generally quiet except for the snoring. One by one people were left at front doors oddly unwilling to open. 'I wasnae' fu' bit jist had plenty,' would be explained.

John was deposited with Stuart, hospitable to the last: 'A wee dram John? For the road?'

'Better not. Better get on, bit late.'

The Land Rover slipped gently from the drive and drove itself along the deserted highway, safely negotiating the tricky bend to reach the river and the bridge which signalled to the coos that the boss was home and would feed them as usual in a few hours' time.

26

Oilman

An early start for John on a day that looked far from promising, a wind rolling dark clouds over the Howe and looking to freshen. Not a day for the North Sea and landing on a rig, but there it was, no telephone call had cancelled. On rising he had looked at the cows: they had chosen to spend the night under cover, a weather forecast well worth noting. Goldwater, who might have preferred to sleep on the brae, raised his head but sighed back into dreamland when it was only the boss leaning against his wall, the known voice telling him all was well.

Charlotte, half asleep, had cooked breakfast and promised several times to check everything again later. She averred that feeding was 'nae bother', she did not mind being left out of the excursion and, with assumed certainty, she could deal with anything that arose. John had done his best to clear the decks for the whole day; no deliveries, no reps, no one from MAFF or about VAT. Nothing of moment should come up yet there remained a knot of anxiety that things would turn awkward for a lone body. 'The readiness is all', William Shakespeare said, but as their friend Wullie knew, 'There's aye a muckle slippy steen at ilka body's door', and even worse, that 'some hae twa'.'

Tric-trac, tric-trac, the planks told the Land Rover was away to a road busy with heavy stuff, 'artics' going north; floats heading to pick up animals for the mart;

201

other wagons so enormous that you had to question their presence on narrow roads. *Cui bono,* this belting progress of loaves of bread or packets of crisps? Not John's, trapped on a leafy stretch approaching Tilly-fourie, regret surfacing for the Alfa, rapid in and out of traffic, the red streak...

Western Oceanic's headquarters in Aberdeen to leave the vehicle before meeting MacB and his secretary to drive to the heliport at Dyce. A smart holdall given to John had his name embroidered on it.

'For me?'

'Yes, with Jerry's compliments!'

It was hard to believe. A great way to mark his day as an oilman: a bright red coverall, the company flag emblazoned across the back, a sleeve with a neat Union Jack badge, a pocket repeated the colour-stitched 'John Grey'. There was a hard hat and rigger boots which explained the request for the 'sayese of his feet'. Charlotte said she told the southern belle, 'Like his head, much, much too big!'

A small helicopter waited on the tarmac but first the reception desk, a signature to give and a video to see on basic survival techniques. Information on the inflatable raft lodged in the cockpit and how to operate it was less than entertaining. In the group of two senior riggers, MacB, secretary Jilly and John, only Jilly accepted the offer of a survival suit. 'They are too awkward, murder to get in and out of, so I don't bother!' Lou said and MacB agreed. Two men on the specialist staff turned Jilly into Michelin Woman while John and the others waited. Remarks were exchanged. John had decided not to bother with a suit.

The helicopter, surprisingly fast along the runway, rose vertically to hover over the airport and wait for clearance. Then out to sea and waves unsuitable for any raft. A buffeting wind but the strong throb of the rotor countered all sound. The rig loomed vast and complex, its landing platform small. Jilly's face paled. Lou and the other rigger were impassive, MacB unreadable. It was familiar to John, tension, the appearance of calm covering knife-edge alertness but a complete reliance on whoever was in charge of an operation. A service thing, each man doing what he was trained for. In this case the pilot would land safely whatever the conditions.

The platform was swathed with thick netting. At touchdown men came running to shackle the machine before the wind could take it. The pilot stopped the rotor. The sea a maelstrom but no risk as they disembarked, someone on hand to steer each person into shelter. Light and warmth in a passageway where coveralls and hard hats were put on. A twenty-minute struggle to free Jilly from the suit, but below in the mess coffee bubbling in a very big Cona.

'On tap twenty-four hours a day,' Lou said. 'Keeps us afloat!' Strange juxtaposition among the wild waves of the North Sea, machines which do not stop in the night hours, gouging the ocean bed or pulsing out coffee, an unceasing flow of the black stuff.

MacB's business had to do with food and while he and Jilly carried out checks of stores, making lists of what to reorder, John was taken on a tour. First to the bridge, enclosed like that of a ship, a steering wheel there for when the rig was on the move. Memorable, the sight of roustabouts operating the drills, sweating, covered in oil, extremely hard, unpleasant work, well-paid no doubt but worthy of respect, not a job for a 'mini-man'. (Classified as such could be people pushing paper about, the work-shy and some politicians. Ranked high, crooks who targeted the innocent and unwary and higher still the 'stars' posturing as they gobbled up a microphone and pretended to sing. A fascinating list with no end to it.)

Finally below, to see through a trapdoor waves pounding against the rig's complex ironwork. So familiar the spray, creamy-white against a darkening swell, the depths challenged now by this colossus. A sharp feeling of nostalgia, almost regret that he had exchanged the sea for a handful of green fields.

Back in the warmth of the mess, goodwill and talk. It emerged that not all visitors were congenial. A tall redheaded man explained.

'This lassie, some wee-bit medical assistant, came on board and er, made a fuss!'

'Panic? I suppose a girl might...'

'Nae! It wisnae panic as such!'

There was obviously more to come, wry grins on some faces, and a hint of laughter.

'She wisnae on board for five minutes...'

'When somebody misbehaved!'

'The whole bloody lot of you misbehaved by the sound of it!'

'You must have seen the papers! Front page in the *Record*.'

'And the *News of the World!*'

It was John's turn to laugh. 'I never see a newspaper, honestly!'

'Weel, she said she wis harassed!' Laughter again.

'Twas the Yank gotten the worst o' it!'

'Yep! Me most of all. Mugshots doing me no favours! But no way I did!' He had a jolly face with injured innocence written all over it. 'Boy, you would have to be crazy! That dame was no oil painting!'

MacB ready for departure and Jilly already fitted into the suit. Goodbyes and thanks. Again the careful escort to the machine. A vertical take-off to another rig, *Pacesetter 2*, to pick up a roustabout going on leave. A safe landing at Dyce. Handshakes and thanks to the pilot, also due to go on leave. In no time at all John was on the way home, mulling over a day to be treasured. Nobody he knew had been offered or ever wanted such a trip. He had relished it: even the helicopter blown and buffeted by the wind. Being at sea again, Memories. The destroyer thumped from the crest of every wave, the tremendous shuddering as if the boat would disintegrate. The rig had been more stable than that, but the sea...

He drove back to Charlotte and the green fields.

This Large Print Book, for people
who cannot read normal print,
is published under the auspices of

THE ULVERSCROFT FOUNDATION

... we hope you have enjoyed this book.
Please think for a moment about those
who have worse eyesight than you ...
and are unable to even read or enjoy
Large Print without great difficulty.

You can help them by sending a
donation, large or small, to:

**The Ulverscroft Foundation,
1, The Green, Bradgate Road,
Anstey, Leicestershire, LE7 7FU,
England.**
or request a copy of our brochure for
more details.

The Foundation will use all donations
to assist those people who are visually
impaired and need special attention
with medical research, diagnosis
and treatment.

Thank you very much for your help.